# NEVERTHELESS
# I LIVE

# NEVERTHELESS I LIVE

## hope for a hurting heart

MONA ADKISSON

TATE PUBLISHING
AND ENTERPRISES, LLC

Published by Tate Publishing & Enterprises, LLC
127 E. Trade Center Terrace | Mustang, Oklahoma 73064 USA
1.888.361.9473 | www.tatepublishing.com

Tate Publishing is committed to excellence in the publishing industry. The company reflects the philosophy established by the founders, based on Psalm 68:11,
*"The Lord gave the word and great was the company of those who published it."*

Book design copyright © 2012 by Tate Publishing, LLC. All rights reserved.
*Cover design by Erin DeMoss*
*Interior design by Christina Hicks*

Published in the United States of America

ISBN: 978-1-62024-156-1
1. Biography & Autobiography / Personal Memoirs
2. Family & Relationships / Death, Grief, Bereavement
12.05.23

# DEDICATION

To my loving husband, Sam, and my oldest son, Adam.

# ACKNOWLEDGMENTS

There are so many people whose contribution I would like to acknowledge. I'm very grateful to Tate Publishing and Dr. Richard and Rita Tate for believing that my story would bring hope and healing to the hearts of many. I would like to thank their staff for working so effectively with a novice. I've learned so much and can honestly say that this experience has been a highlight in my journey of faith.

I would like to give a special thanks to Shaunti Feldhan for taking the time to keep a divine appointment. Her encouragement gave me the confidence to take the next step and her staff offered wisdom and insight that affirmed my mission.

My precious daughter-in-law, Tiffany, offered invaluable insight as she helped me work through some of the difficult subject matter of this book. Her consistent support was such a blessing, and I'll forever be thankful that God brought her into my life.

I would like to acknowledge my son Chase's classmates; many of whom are graduating from college this year; Casady Fletcher, Janna Smith, Laruen Forgety, Krista Green, Dalton Coates, Emily Yates, Chelsea Watters, Cody Mitchell, Brittany Chambless, P.K.

Shelb, Rachel Allison, Jessica Stevens, and Zachary Melton. Because Chase "graduated" early, I often needed an extra smile or a warm hug which many of you graciously provided.

Most of all, I would like to thank everyone who had a part in the lives of my children: the Sunday School teachers, who took the time to teach them to love the Lord, and my church family, who allowed them to grow up in a loving environment.

To all of the family and friends who loved my children, I say, "Thank you."

# TABLE OF CONTENTS

# INTRODUCTION

How do I begin to explain why I chose to write this book? I can only say that God's gentle nudging and my husband Sam's persistent encouragement wouldn't let our story go untold. Sam firmly believes that our experiences can help other people who are walking through grief themselves or those who want to help someone they know.

It is typical for people who have lost someone to search for a way to memorialize them. It helps to feel that the legacy of their loved one will live on. I personally feared that my memories would fade, and I struggled to find a way to capture those precious memories, so I was compelled to write poems about my children. I never planned to write a book about our experiences, but through the years, many people have encouraged me to do this.

With no writing experience or preparation for this kind of task, I refer to myself as a reluctant author. I attempted to start the writing process several times but didn't really make progress until recently. It seemed that each time I would begin writing, something would happen to distract me or I wouldn't feel the freedom to write. When I finally got down to the most intense parts of my story, I spent a week—by myself—recording the details. It was emotionally draining because I had to relive each of the events precisely as they had happened. Experiencing the emotions again triggered the grief as strongly as I had felt it at the time. Tears flowed as I replayed the events in my mind and then on paper.

The title, *Nevertheless, I Live*, was taken from Galatians 2:19-21, "I am crucified with Christ: nevertheless I live; yet not I, but Christ liveth in me: and the life which I now live in the flesh I live by faith in the Son of God, who loved me, and gave himself for me." As you will see, God spoke to me through this verse in a very special way.

Loss is an inevitable part of life, but most people are not prepared to cope with grief. Many people feel a sense of hopelessness and despair when they are hurting from a difficult marriage, betrayal, financial reversal, sickness, or after losing someone they love. If people can gain a sense of hope as they read how we made it through trying circumstances, we will feel that something good has come from our grief. Then, just maybe, they will share that hope with others.

My family survived our tragedies by the grace of God and the love and support of friends and family. Some people are not blessed to have that love and support, so my prayer is that our story will encourage and hopefully inspire others to place their lives and their circumstances in the hands of God and that he would reveal himself to them in tangible ways, just as he has done for me. He is faithful and will not leave them even in their time of need. I hope that those who read this book will grow closer to God if they have a relationship with him, and if they have never placed their faith in God through Jesus Christ, that they will come to know him in a personal way.

# BEAUTIFUL BOYS

As a girl, I envisioned what it would be like to grow up and marry the man of my dreams. My childhood years were less than perfect. So my dreams were quickly brought into check by reality. The fact was that no matter what I conjured up in my imagination, men were just not very reliable. Maybe that's why it took my dear husband of thirty years so long to win my trust. We met in 1978 while I was working in the office of admissions at the University of Oklahoma. After dating off and on for two years, we married on June 28, 1980.

I fell in love with Sam because he was the first man in my life to demonstrate unconditional love for me. He was the most affectionate person I had ever been around in my life! It was almost embarrassing, especially for someone like me, who had never received that kind of attention from a man. Sam couldn't carry a tune in a bucket, but that didn't stop him from singing love songs to me. He was unabashed in his attempts to win my heart. I look back over those early years of marriage and realize just how sincere he was. Often my perception was clouded by my mistrust of men, stemming from some unfortunate childhood experiences. My sister and I were raised by a divorced, working mother with no father.

Never having had a healthy relationship with men, my mother painted a very distorted picture of what marriage would be like. For most of my young life, my mother dated a married man. He finally divorced after I graduated high school and married my mother when I was twenty-five years old. We had always known him as "Christie," which is his last name. Suddenly he was my stepfather. I wanted my mother to be happy, but I had mixed emotions about their marriage as memories of their volatile relationship were etched in my mind. Sam, on the other hand, had been raised by two loving parents who had stayed together through thick and thin.

I'll never forget how excited Sam and I were when we learned we were expecting our first child. We had been married for about two years. Sam's sister, Donna, worked in the lab of Norman Regional Hospital, and I went there to have a blood sample taken.

After she drew my blood she said, "Call me in a couple of hours, and I should have the results."

So, I did what most of us women love to do—I went to the mall! As I shopped I kept a close eye on my watch, and as soon as two hours were up, I called Donna from a pay-phone. I could hear the excitement in her voice when she announced, "The test was positive!"

I could not believe it! It was both exciting and scary. The thought of raising a child brought back memories of the mistakes my parents had made. There was no way I was going to make those same mistakes—or would I? Not having grown up around children other than my younger sister, I didn't know the first thing about raising a child, much less about taking care of a baby; I was scared to death.

When I got home later that day, it was time to give Sam the good news. He was so happy! He grabbed me and lifted me off the floor, and as he swung me around, he said, "We're gonna have a baby, darlin'! I'm so proud of you!" Then he rubbed my tummy and began talking to the baby. We had not planned this pregnancy, but we were as ready as we could be. Most of us never think we have enough time or money to raise children, but the thought of passing on a part of oneself to another generation is irresistible. When I had dreamed of my future husband, occasionally I would also dare to dream of children. I prayed that my baby would be a dark-haired, blue-eyed baby boy who looked just like his daddy. Since God had already fulfilled my dream of a loving husband, I knew anything was possible.

On May 2, 1983, our beautiful baby boy was born. Sam was right there with me in the delivery room, and as soon as he saw that the baby was a boy he started yelling, "It's a boy! I got a boy!" as he ran down the hall to tell our families. Soon Sam was back and helped the nurse weigh the baby and clean him up.

He then proudly announced, "He weighs seven pounds, seven ounces! That's what I weighed when I was born!"

I couldn't believe my eyes when our baby arrived in the very package that I had dreamed of. His hair was almost black, his eyes were dark blue, and best of all, he was healthy. What a blessing! After much thought, we named him Samuel Adam Adkisson. The name Samuel was chosen for two reasons. First, because it's a name that has been passed down for several generations in the Adkisson family. Secondly, it was a biblical name. Both of these reasons were important to me. Having a strong tie to family was especially significant, because I had never had that in my own life. I wanted our son to feel connected to his father's family history. Also, I wanted our son to know the legacy of the biblical patriarchs. I had not grown up in a Christian home, but I was determined to raise my children with a firm foundation in biblical truth.

I didn't know the first thing about being a wife or a mother. My own mother and sister joked that they were afraid to leave me alone with my baby.

My sister called and asked my mother, "Are you sure she'll know what to do with him?" Much to their amazement, Adam not only survived, he thrived. My maternal instincts kicked in, and we were off to the races!

After Adam was born, my thirst for spiritual knowledge became unquenchable. I instinctively knew that I wanted to raise my children in a Christian home, unlike the dysfunctional environment that I grew up in. I began searching for information about how to raise children and how to have a Christian marriage. There was a new Bible study called Philosophy of Christian Womanhood being offered at a local church. It sounded like just what I needed. They even had a nursery so I could take my baby with me. The study lasted twenty-seven weeks, and I attended faithfully. I can honestly say that experience changed my life. I met my friend, Margo, there, and we're friends to this day. The truths that I learned in that Bible study from Scripture had a profound impact on me.

I learned what the Bible had to say about the relationship between a husband and wife. I learned that our marriage was vitally important to giving our children stability and security. These were things that I never had as a child. I was bound and determined to give my child the solid foundation that had been so lacking in my own life. I had become a Christian at the age of fourteen and realized that there was a much better life available to us when we allowed God to shape us and mold us into his likeness. I was hearing things in this Bible study that I had never heard before. Maybe it was possible to trust a man if we both loved God and practiced these biblical teachings about marriage.

I also learned what the word *submission* meant in a biblical sense. It's a gift that we choose to give someone out of love and respect. My whole attitude toward my husband changed after learning this concept. Instead of feeling controlled and manipulated, I began to see my husband as the spiritual leader of our home. Sam was human, and even though he fell short at times, I took comfort in knowing that he was accountable to God. Sam loved for me to go to Bible study because I always came home with a warm heart toward him. He would always remind me, "You don't want to be late for your Bible study!" Gradually, I was learning to trust and love my husband unconditionally.

We enjoyed Adam so much, and by the time he was two, we discovered that I was pregnant with our second child. Sam and Adam were so excited! Sam was envisioning a football team, and Adam was just happy because everybody else was happy. When he learned he was going to be a big brother, the first thing he wanted to do was call Mimie, the name he affectionately called my mother.

This time, I chose to find out if the baby was a boy or a girl. Much to my husband's delight, the doctor was about seventy-five percent sure it was another boy. We would have the start of a football team! I must confess, another dark-haired, blue-eyed boy would fit just fine in my dreams.

Not long after we found out I was pregnant, we discovered that Sam's dad's lung cancer had returned. He had to have another serious surgery and radiation therapy. I remember some very precious times together when I drove him to receive his treatments. Unfortunately, my father-in-law never got to see our second child. Sam's dad had a stroke on Thanksgiving Day and had to go back to the hospital. I was six months pregnant at the time, and I remember standing beside his bed and him rubbing my tummy when he was too weak to say what he felt. I said, "You're going to have another grandson." The look in his eyes said it all. He was so proud of us. Sadly, he only lived a few more days.

Such is the substance of life. Children are born, and parents pass away. Bills still have to be paid, diapers have to be changed, and meals have to be prepared. But none of us were prepared for the impact that losing Sam's dad would have on our family. Sam's mother, Bonnie, was devastated. Having been stricken with polio at the age of twenty-three while she was pregnant with Sam, she had walked on crutches for years. It wasn't until the last few years that she had become totally dependent upon a wheelchair. She often said, "My husband never makes me feel handicapped." But now he was gone, and she struggled with loneliness and depression. She stayed with us for a couple of weeks, and then Sam wisely made the decision that she needed to go home and learn to adjust. It wasn't going to get any easier. She was only fifty-four years old, and she had many years of life ahead of her.

Feeling overwhelmed with the pressures of trying to meet all of our needs, Sam chose to bury himself in his work. We spent the last few weeks of my pregnancy struggling to maintain balance in our relationship. His mother was still grieving and needed his time and attention, and so did Adam and I.

There were a few slight complications with my second pregnancy. The baby's heartbeat was a little slow, so I had to be monitored periodically. But other than that and a little morning sickness, things proceeded normally. My due date came and went without as much as a false alarm. I remember walking up and down the hill on our street because I had heard it would help start my contractions. Unfortunately, it didn't work. I was due on January 30, and the baby didn't arrive until February 10. He chose to make his appearance right in the middle of a huge snowstorm. Sam had to drive me to the hospital in his four-wheel drive pickup.

He assured me, "I can deliver the baby on the side of the road if we get stranded."

I said, "Wow! That really makes me feel better!" Sam loved to tease me because he always knew he would get a reaction.

We did make it to the hospital without sliding into the ditch, and Bradley Edward Adkisson was born later that afternoon. He was exactly the way I had pictured him: another beautiful baby boy with dark hair and blue eyes. He was the picture of health. God had truly blessed us a second time. I thought Sam had acted excited when Adam was born, but you should have heard him yell this time.

"It's a boy! I've got another boy! Yeah!" Would you believe that Bradley weighed seven pounds, seven ounces, just like Adam and Sam had?

Life was good. We grew as a family, and we grew closer to the Lord. My expectations about marriage had been exceeded, even through some difficult times. I've often thought that God must have a great sense of humor. Here I was raising a family of boys when I had grown up with all women! Much to my surprise, not only were these guys okay, they were great!

# LIVING LIFE

Our joy over Brad's arrival was diminished by the sadness of losing Sam's dad. His mother continued to have a very difficult time dealing with the loss of her husband and became clinically depressed. We had some dark days dealing with her loneliness and grief.

Being in our twenties, we had never lost anyone close to us; therefore, we had no idea how to handle grief and the fallout of emotion that accompanied such a loss. We were overwhelmed with the responsibility of raising a two-year-old, adjusting to a new baby, coping with the loss of a parent, and the depression Sam's mother was experiencing. As if that weren't enough, our income was cut in half due to a major decline in oil prices that devastated Sam's industry.

This was truly a difficult time in our relationship. Sam felt pulled between a sense of responsibility for his mother and the need to provide for a family. He couldn't handle the emotional episodes with his mother, so he just avoided them as much as possible. This only made matters worse. She blamed me for keeping him away, and I spent most of my time crying because I felt abandoned. What had happened to our marriage? We had begun to grow so close in recent years, but now we hardly talked without fighting. At times I felt like our marriage was over. I would say, "Honey, can we talk about what's going on with your mother?"

He would get defensive and say, "I can't please either one of you! There isn't enough of me to go around, and I feel like you two are pulling me apart!"

Often he would leave the house to avoid a fight.

I felt isolated because I didn't want to tell anyone how bad things were. I do remember reaching out to my friend, Paula, who had lost both of her parents. Her words were comforting and gave me strength. She said, "Talk to the Lord about your problems, Mona. Continue to pray, and read God's Word. He is always there for you and will give you wisdom and strength." It felt good just to tell another person what was going on.

Sam did a lot of fishing during that time. I think he just had to get away from all of the problems at home. Of course, it only made things worse for me because I was home with a two-year-old and a newborn. I loved breastfeeding, but it was very demanding, and I was so tired. Sam's mother would call at all hours of the day and night because she was lonely and scared. The phone might ring at 2:00 a.m., and Bonnie would say to Sam, "I need you! Come over here right now. If you loved me, you would care and not leave me alone!"

Sam would say, "I do love you, and I'm sorry you're lonely. I know you miss Dad. I'll come see you tomorrow."

These conversations sometimes lasted a few minutes, and sometimes they lasted for an hour or more.

Looking back, I'm sure she felt totally abandoned. We couldn't meet our own needs, much less hers. Years later, she said, "We were like two sick people trying to help each other get well." Neither of us had the strength to help ourselves, and we certainly didn't have the strength to help one another.

We struggled along for two years or more. Sam never had time to grieve his father's death. He was too busy trying to keep his head above water financially and trying to keep his family from falling apart. He did look forward to coming home at the end of the day and seeing his boys. They would hear his pickup pull into the driveway, and they would go running to the back door yelling, "Dad's home! Dad's home!"

Sam would always pause outside the door as they pulled the curtain back to make sure it was him then he would burst in and grab the boys up and toss them around. He would say, "How's my partner?" to Brad, and he would hold him high up in the air as Brad giggled with delight. Adam would want to wrestle on the floor until time for supper.

I felt like an outsider sometimes because things weren't right between us as husband and wife. Sam enjoyed the boys so much, but things were very tense between him and me.

There were some happy times, though. For me, those moments came during the day when I was able to enjoy the boys without Sam around. I have some wonderful videos of the boys when they were little. I was big on body parts. I would often ask, "Where are your eyes?" "Where are your toes?" "Where is your belly button?" My two little geniuses hardly missed a one. It's so funny to look at those tapes now. It's also boring for everyone but the parents. There is one precious tape of Brad singing "Jesus Loves Me." It is priceless. Those beautiful blue eyes are so innocent, and his little face is angelic as he bursts into the refrain.

Things did gradually improve in our marriage. We learned to avoid discussing certain topics, and as a result we fought less. But we also never resolved the underlying issues.

When Brad was two years old, I was happy that having his big brother made him easier to potty train. I placed a jar of M&M's on the back of the toilet, and he got one for number one and two for number two. It had worked well with Adam, and it was a breeze with Brad because he wanted to be just like his big brother!

The boys loved to build forts. Often I would hang sheets over the dining room table, and they would climb around in there for hours. As most little boys do, they loved to play outside. Adam liked Rambo and would often put an army hat on Brad, his second in command, and they would pretend they were in the jungle. By the end of the day, they would be filthy!

By that summer, I was ready to spend some time outside myself. I didn't have a car at the time, but being the resourceful person that I am, I loaded the boys into Sam's one-ton flatbed truck and took them to our pond to fish. The truck had a manual gearshift, and I had to maneuver it around Brad's car seat to change gears, but it worked. I bought a bucket of minnows, and we headed out. When we got there, Adam was dying to fish, so I baited his hook and helped him get it into the water. As I turned around to check on Brad, he had both hands in the minnow bucket squeezing the minnows! I spent most of my time trying to keep him out of the pond, but Adam and I did manage to catch a stringer of fish. After a couple of hours, I loaded the boys up and we headed back to town.

Sam was playing golf, but I wanted him to see the fish we caught. So I drove by the golf course and happened to catch up with him. He came over to the truck and was amazed at our catch. I could see the pride in his eyes as he looked at his little family. Some of his golf buddies came over to see what was going on, and as we drove away they stood there in amazement that I was able to drive that big old truck with those two kids. I think they were most amazed that I took them fishing and actually caught enough for supper! Sam loved it!

As I drove away he said, "Get those fish cleaned, and I'll be there to eat supper in a little while." His buddies just shook their heads.

That fall was especially fun because Adam and Brad were old enough to enjoy watching football with Sam. They couldn't stay still for long, but they loved to yell when OU scored! By the time basketball season rolled around, Brad was a pro at yelling for his team. You could hear him all over the house, "Go Stacey! Go Stacey! as Stacey King would score.

By the third year of Brad's life, we were regaining some sense of normalcy. Sam's work had picked up, Adam was almost six, and Sam's mother was able to cope a little better. I was still concerned that Sam hadn't been able to grieve over the loss of his dad, but we were functioning better overall. I remember thinking how good it felt to laugh and look forward to the days ahead. It seemed that we were finally climbing out of the valley. Only God knows how and when he is preparing us for life's experiences. If we had known what was ahead, we might have given up hope. God wants us to trust him day by day for the strength we need, and he gives us the grace to handle trials as we need it.

When March rolled around, my mother and sister came to spend spring break with us. We took a trip to Enid, Oklahoma, to see Christie's mother in the nursing home. Adam was old enough to understand, but I wasn't sure how Brad would handle being around old people. Amazingly, he was perfectly comfortable! He even walked down the hallway past each room, smiling and waving at them, saying, "I love you!" You should have seen them smile at his angelic expression!

We stayed with Christie's sister, Mildred, while we were in Enid and enjoyed hearing her tell stories about her life. As my sister, Tara, and I were looking at pictures of Mildred when she was young. Tara asked me, "Have you ever noticed how much you look like Mildred?" We talked about how much she and I resembled one another, even though we weren't related. After staying with Mildred a couple of nights, we headed back to Seminole. The new mall in Shawnee was having a grand opening, and we wanted to take the kids there. We had a great time together, but they had to return to Arkansas that weekend.

As always, my mother was sad about having to leave. She loved my children so much and didn't get to see them nearly as often as she would have liked. Adam was getting so big, and Brad loved to be her "sweet baby." If he got the least little bump or bruise, he would run to Mimie looking at her with those big blue eyes, and of course, she would pick him up and hold him close. Brad would just melt into her arms and look so pitiful. Mother ate it up, and by the time she left, he was ruined!

# NOT ONLY THE STRONG SURVIVE

That Wednesday evening, Adam, Brad, and I ate dinner at church, as usual. Adam had been dedicated to the Lord when he was only nine days old. Brad was dedicated as well. I took them to church every time the doors were open, because I wanted them to learn to trust God. The church had become a very integral part of our lives. I loved the church, and I wanted my boys to love it too. Sam usually attended on Sunday morning but was often working on Wednesday nights when we ate supper there. I looked forward to those meals—no cooking or cleaning up, and I got to be with adults! After the meal, the children had classes to attend, and I went to Bible study.

The boys finished eating, and Adam asked if he could take Brad to the nursery on his way to class. I kissed both boys good-bye and said, "I love you," as they turned and walked away. Brad looked back at me and said, "I love you, Mommy." I thought how precious those words were as I took a mental picture of my two boys. I felt like the luckiest woman in the world.

A few minutes later, I heard a commotion and turned to see what was happening. I saw the door swing open as a friend of mine, Holly, came running into the fellowship hall. She appeared to be distraught, and I could tell something was terribly wrong. She was carrying a child in her arms. I thought, *Oh, no, a child has been hurt.* And then I saw the tennis shoes the child was wearing. That was my child! I ran toward her to see what was wrong. She handed Brad to me, and I looked into his face. I could tell that he was unconscious, and my heart began to race. I started praying, but the only words I could say were, "Oh, God. Oh, God. Oh, God."

By an act of God's grace, our family doctor, Gus, happened to be in the room. He hadn't planned to be there, but his wife, Carol, had needed help carrying in some things. He decided to stay for dinner and was sitting at a table nearby. Gus came running over, and as I handed Bradley to him, I felt my little boy sigh. I said, "Oh, good, he's breathing!" Gus took Brad and laid him on the floor and began trying to revive him. I remember seeing Adam out of the corner of my eye. He had come into the fellowship hall to see what was happening. Virgil—one of the deacons—took him by the hand and led him outside. Some of my friends gathered around me and took me into the next room to sit down. I could feel myself hyperventilating. I didn't know what was wrong with Brad, but I had a terrible feeling in my stomach. I remember seeing the vanilla-colored walls and hearing the hum of a vending machine as the women surrounded me and began praying. They prayed that the doctor would be able to help Brad.

They prayed for me and Sam and Adam. They even prayed that the person who went to find Sam would be able to reach him without delay. I remember praying, "God! Please don't let him die!" I don't know how long we were in the room. Time just seemed to stand still.

Sam arrived very quickly. Almost as if God had planned it, he had been at home and was not out on a job. My husband looked at me and asked, "What happened? Mona, tell me what happened!" I tried to explain what I knew, but it didn't make much sense.

Someone came through the door and told us, "They're calling an ambulance."

I remember feeling so cold and scared as Sam said, "Good, we'll get him to the hospital, and he'll be okay."

The ambulance arrived, and Brad was taken out on a stretcher. One of the men from church rode in the ambulance with him as Sam and I followed the ambulance to the hospital in our truck. We were terrified, but Sam just kept saying, "He'll be okay, Mona. He probably hit his head or something. He'll be okay."

I said, "He's dead. I know he's dead."

Sam wouldn't let me say that. He said, "No, Mona, he's going to be okay."

We arrived at the emergency room and were ushered into a waiting area. I don't remember much except just feeling very cold and sick to my stomach. I tried to pray, but words wouldn't come, and thoughts were swirling through my brain. I felt like I was living a nightmare.

Gradually, people from church began arriving. They tried to comfort us as best they could, "We're praying that Brad will be okay, Mona." Sam and I just sat there, staring blankly, for what seemed like an eternity. At one point, I remember choking out these words to our pastor, "I can't pray."

He wisely responded, "That's okay. God understands." The memory of a scripture passage flooded into my heart and mind. Romans 8:26 (NIV) says, "We do not know what we ought to pray for, but the Spirit himself intercedes for us with groans that words cannot express." Even in such a time as this, God provides.

Finally, Gus came out to talk to us. He had a very stern look on his face. We had known this man for a long time, and we could tell something was very wrong. I was thinking to myself, *Okay, I can handle this. If my son is a paraplegic, I'll just take care of him. I'll sit by his bed. I'll feed him. The Lord will give me the strength to do whatever I have to do.* I was resigned to the news. When Gus spoke, the words that came out of his mouth were astounding. He told us that our son was dead—that Brad had a broken neck. I felt like someone had punched me in the stomach! I wasn't expecting this. Sam and I just broke down and wept. We were in total shock.

"I want to see him! Where is my son? I want to see Brad," I told Gus. He led us into the room where our son lay on an examination table. I could smell the scent of anesthetic as my eyes surveyed the room. I couldn't believe how still my three-year-old son was. It was immediately apparent that Brad was no longer occupying that body. His spirit was gone. We spent a few moments gazing through our tears at the little shell that lay before us. I tried to memorize every inch of his small frame, especially his hands and feet. His skin was cold. I had never felt anything like that before. Sam and I spent a few minutes with our son; I kissed Brad on the forehead for the last time, and we turned and walked toward the door. I turned back for one last look, and Sam said, "Come on, darlin'," but I lingered a moment longer not wanting to open that door.

"Let's stay a little longer," I cried. "I don't want to leave him alone."

Sam gently pulled me by the arm, "It's time to go, honey. There's nothing else we can do." As I walked through that door I felt like I was walking through a looking glass like *Alice in Wonderland*. Nothing seemed real.

From that point on, my memories are foggy. We walked through the hospital waiting area lined with people. I remember looking at them and seeing the reflection of our own pain on their faces. I had never felt so helpless. Each one would give us a hug or express some words of comfort in their attempt to help us as we walked by. I felt like we were in a parade as we passed through the crowd. My legs felt like they were stuck in molasses, and everything was happening in slow motion. It felt strange having all those eyes gazing at us, but it was also comforting to have people who cared surrounding us. Sam and I made our way outside to his truck. As we drove home, we were only beginning to realize how very different our world was from just a few short hours ago.

As we walked into our house, people from the church began arriving. We asked someone where Adam was. We were told that some friends who had a child his age had taken him home with them. They planned to let him spend the night. I was relieved that I didn't have to face Adam right away. How were we going to tell him what had happened? He was only five years old. It was hard enough facing what had happened ourselves, but to lose one child and then face shattering the innocence of another was more than we could bear. We did call Adam on the phone. He asked if Brad was okay. We told him we weren't sure, and we would talk about it tomorrow.

Family members had to be called. I remember Gus's wife, Carol, saying to me, "Mona, you need to call your mother." I finally made the call and shattered one more world.

People stayed until late that night, and when Sam and I went to bed, we were exhausted. We fell into a deep sleep and finally escaped the nightmare.

I awoke to the sound of birds chirping outside my window as I stretched and let out a yawn. My first thought was, *What a wonderful sound. The sun is shining, and it is going to be a beautiful day.* The thought had barely crossed my mind when I felt a ton of bricks land right in the middle of my chest. My stomach drew into a knot, and hot tears began streaming down my cheeks. I could feel sound coming from my throat, but the noise I was making wasn't recognizable. It can only be described as a moan that began deep in my spirit and escaped from my mouth without translation. I remember hearing this moaning, and I knew it was coming from inside of me, but I couldn't stop it. Sam tried to comfort me as best he could. But every time I looked into his eyes, I saw the raw pain in his heart.

The first person I remember coming into our room was my friend, Cynthia. She sat beside me on the bed and put her arms around me. As she held me, she whispered in my ear, "My grace is sufficient for you…" 2 Corinthians 12:9 (NIV). My thoughts immediately turned to the Lord, and I could feel my mind searching for the solid rock of Scripture. The Bible promises that God will not leave us or forsake us in times of trouble. This was a real turning point for me. I think I realized the choices I would make in the days ahead would affect my relationship with Christ forever.

Cynthia always says that we have to keep an "eternal perspective." That wasn't easy to do when my whole world was falling apart. But I guess that's when we prove what we believe. Will God meet all of our needs, and does he care about all of the details of our lives? Is he a loving God who won't put more on us than we can handle? Well, I guessed I would find out, but I wasn't sure I had enough faith to sustain me. All I knew was that I loved the Lord with all my heart.

The first thing Sam and I had to do was go to Adam. We had to decide how to tell him. We drove to where he was and took him into a room by himself. I could tell he was anxious as he came running over to us and said, "How's Brad?"

Sam sat him on one knee and held him close as he said, "Adam, Brad is in heaven with Jesus."

Tears ran down our son's face as the realization that his brother wasn't coming home sank in. I was down on my knees holding them both as Adam asked, "What happened to him?"

Sam said, "Brad hit his head really hard when he fell."

Sam and I tried to answer his questions honestly but without too many details. We didn't want to scare him any more than he already was. Adam cried a little, and we talked some more, but soon he wanted to get down and play. We thanked our friends for keeping him overnight as we gathered up our son and went home.

Family members began arriving later that day. We had to relive the events that led up to Brad's death over and over. Brad had been walking into the church nursery, smiling and laughing. He was strutting in his usual manner when suddenly he just fell face down on the floor. He didn't try to catch himself. Those who saw it said he just fell like a board. The nursery workers gathered around and must have thought at first that he was playing. When he didn't move, Holly picked him up, and when she couldn't get him to respond, she began running to where we were in the fellowship hall. That was all we knew. There were so many unanswered questions. What caused him to fall? Could anyone have saved him? Why did he not catch himself when he fell?

We didn't have time to dwell on those questions because there were details to be worked out, and plans had to be made. People graciously offered their homes for my family to stay in, and food arrived by the droves.

# IN MY FATHER'S HOUSE

Having planned his father's funeral, Sam knew what had to be done. I was amazed at his strength as he went about taking care of the many details.

Sam spoke to the funeral director about planning the service, and then he proceeded to work on making the funeral arrangements and purchasing a cemetery plot. Maybe it helped him to have something he could control. I just remember picking out the casket and the floral spray that would be placed on top. It felt so strange to flip through pictures of casket sprays. But I knew what I wanted. I told the funeral director, "I want a spring bouquet with tiny pink rosebuds." It seemed appropriate for such a young life that had never been allowed to bloom.

As we walked past the many caskets, Sam said, "Honey, I think this one is perfect." It was white with gold trim, and it was the smallest one I had ever seen.

I felt a painful stab in my heart as I said, "Yes, that one is perfect."

We also had to choose songs and find someone to sing, which was difficult because no one thought they could possibly sing without breaking down. We finally asked some dear friends, and they agreed to try. My friend, Karen, offered to take pictures and video the memorial service. I wasn't sure it was appropriate but accepted her offer because I wanted to preserve as much of my son's memory as I possibly could. Our pastor, Brother Bob Hammons, was on hand to help plan the service. He wisely guided us through some difficult decisions. There was so much that had to be done, and all Sam and I wanted to do was wake up and find out it had all been a very bad dream.

As we considered the songs that would be sung at Brad's memorial, friends made suggestions that must have been inspired by God—each one had such meaning. Our friend, Owen Melton, came by and said, "'Because He Lives' fits this situation because it assures us that God will help us face tomorrow."

As we read the words, we agreed that the message it spoke was perfect. Sam and I chose "Peace in the Valley" because it talks about being led by a little child. We decided to ask Holly to sing and play her guitar because her sweet voice and the simple strum of her guitar seemed so appropriate for a child's memorial. As we talked to each person who was to sing, their response was the same: "I'll do my best to make it through."

Brother Bob talked to us about the order of service, and we agreed that the memorial should focus on the hope that we have of seeing our son again and pointing others to Christ. In my heart, I wondered how that could be done under such sad circumstances. Children aren't supposed to die suddenly, for no apparent reason. How would God be glorified through that? Our thoughts bounced between praise to God for not allowing Brad to suffer, anger over having to live the rest of our lives broken by such a harsh reality, and confusion over why God would allow such a thing to happen to an innocent child.

In the midst of the preparations for the funeral, Gus came to see us. He said, "I would like to send Brad's body to the State Medical Examiner for an autopsy."

I cried as I listened to Gus's request.

Sam said, "Well, I guess that's the only way we'll ever know what really happened to our son."

After some discussion, we gave our permission to allow the autopsy. But later, the realization of what we had agreed to began to sink in. Our son's body was going to be violated by a radical surgical procedure. How could we allow our three-year-old to go through any more trauma? Hadn't his little body been through enough? My protective instincts made me regret the decision. I saw in my mind images of what would actually be done to our little boy's body. This was the ultimate offense! As I tried to reason it out in my mind, Sam and I discussed it. "This is the only way we will get any answers about what happened, Mona."

My voice broke as I said, "But how will it affect the funeral arrangements? Would we still be able to bury him right away? If so, the State Medical Examiner would have to do the autopsy on Friday and get Brad's body back to us in time for the funeral on Saturday."

We realized there wasn't enough time for that to happen, so it was determined that we would have the service on Saturday and rather than burying our son, his body would be taken to Oklahoma City for the autopsy. As soon as the procedure was finished, Brad's body would be brought back for burial. This could take several days.

There was an unending flow of people in our home. Many women from church were there to do the routine chores. It was their way of ministering to us. What a humbling experience to watch people wash my dishes, mop my floors, and scrub my bathrooms. I joked, "God is punishing me for not being a better housekeeper! He is allowing you all to see my dirt!" Watching people interrupt their daily lives to come and surround us with such love was overwhelming. God provided for all of our needs. People seemed to feel better if they were able to help in some way. It was almost as if they needed to work through their own grief. When a child dies so suddenly, people sense the fragility of life. It brings us all in touch with our own mortality and the realization that even the young are appointed once to die. There was an unspoken question on everyone's lips: "How could God allow this to happen?"

We had decided that Adam would stay with Carol and her son instead of coming to the service because Sam and I would be doing well to manage our own emotions. We were afraid Adam would be traumatized by seeing his parents emotional and upset. As ironic as it seems, the doctor who administered medical care to Brad was helping to care for Adam, watching over Sam and me, and was a pallbearer at the funeral. But that's what Christians do. They see a need and allow God to use them to meet that need. The Bible instructs us to carry one another's burdens. We were witnesses to that kind of love.

The day of the funeral, family members arrived at our house early. As time for the service approached, I felt an overwhelming desire to gather everyone together and pray. Some of our family members were not Christians, and Sam and I wanted them to witness the faith that was holding us together. Sam said, "Gather around, everyone. We want Brother Bob to say a prayer. Mona and I are so grateful to you all for coming and being here for us." We formed a large circle in the living room, and our pastor led us in prayer. That may have been the first time some of them had prayed in a long time, if ever.

The funeral cars arrived to take us to the church. As we entered the funeral car, I felt like I was walking through a dream. This couldn't really be happening to me. We were going to see our son for the last time. In the span of an hour, we would review our son's short life, take one last look at his body, and tell him good-bye—forever. It just didn't seem right.

The family stayed in a holding room until the service began. We were escorted into the church auditorium, and as we walked toward the front of the church, I could see people crying all around us. The church was almost full. I could hear beautiful music playing and a trio of our friends singing a familiar song that was very special to us—"I can feel the brush of angels' wings; I see glory on each face. / Surely the presence of the Lord is in this place."

When we got close to the front, I saw the tiny casket, and my heart almost stopped beating! I thought I was going to pass out. Gus had given me a Xanax earlier, so I felt groggy and was glad when I felt the pew underneath me. There were beautiful flowers everywhere. The spray on the casket was just perfect. It did seem appropriate for a child who hadn't completed the first stages of life.

We had hoped that the service would be a celebration of Bradley's young life. We wanted people to know that our faith in Christ was strong, and it was that faith that was getting us through this event. It was important to us that Bradley be remembered for his precious life rather than for his untimely death. As the service began, Sam and I quietly prayed, "Dear Lord, may every aspect of this service point people to faith and hope rather than highlight the devastation we feel from the loss of our precious son."

Brother Bob introduced our neighbor, Vicki, who read a beautiful poem entitled "To All Parents" by Edgar A. Guest. It tells how God chooses special parents to raise a particular child, and how we are given the responsibility of training that child. It also speaks of the brevity of life. "He'll bring his charms to gladden you, and shall his stay be brief, /You'll have his lovely memories as solace for your grief." Then this beautiful poem prays for God's will to be done, even when we are left wondering why.

Brother Bob quoted John 14:1-3, 7 (KJV),

Let not your heart be troubled: ye believe in God, believe also in me. In my Father's house are many mansions: if it were not so, I would have told you. I go to prepare a place for you. And if I go and prepare a place for you, I will come again, and receive you unto myself; that where I am, there ye may be also. Peace I leave with you, my peace I give unto you; not as the world giveth, give I unto you. Let not your heart be troubled, neither let it be afraid.

Then he quietly sat down as Janice walked to the microphone. We had asked her to sing "Peace in the Valley" because we loved her voice and knew she would bring the song to life, as it told the story of how we will all be changed as we pass from this life to the next. "And the beasts from the wild, shall be led by a little child, / and I'll be changed, changed from this creature that I am, oh yes." We were not disappointed as Janice poured her heart out in song.

As our pastor approached the pulpit to begin his remarks, his voice cracked with emotion. Brother Bob had been a pastor for over forty years and had preached many funerals, but this was obviously a difficult moment for him. His words were soothing as he quoted familiar passages from the Bible. I had heard them many times before, but they took on new meaning as they were spoken over my son's lifeless body.

And they brought young children to him, that he should touch them: and his disciples rebuked those that brought them. But when Jesus saw it, he was much displeased, and said unto them,

Suffer the little children to come unto me, and forbid them not: for of such is the kingdom of God. Verily I say unto you, Whosoever shall not receive the kingdom of God as a little child, he shall not enter therein. And he took them up in his arms, put his hands upon them, and blessed them.

Mark 10:13-16 (KJV)

At the same time came the disciples unto Jesus, saying, Who is the greatest in the kingdom of heaven? And Jesus called a little child unto him, and set him in the midst of them, and said, verily I say unto you, except ye be converted, and become as little children, ye shall not enter into the kingdom of heaven. Whosoever therefore shall humble himself as this little child, the same is greatest in the kingdom of heaven. And whoso shall receive one such little child in my name receiveth me.

Matthew 18:1-5 (KJV)

"Take heed that ye despise not one of these little ones; for I say unto you, That in heaven their angels do always behold the face of my Father which is in heaven" Matthew 18:10 (KJV). Then Brother Bob paused as Holly stepped to the microphone. She softly strummed her guitar and began singing the simple verses of a familiar children's medley, "Praise him, praise him all ye little children. God is love, God is love / Jesus loves the little children! All the children of the world / Jesus loves me this I know, for the Bible tells me so.

People were openly weeping, and it was obvious they had been deeply touched by the message of those simple songs. As he stepped back to the microphone, Brother Bob prayed, "Our Father, I remember one time when there was a storm, and Jesus said, 'Peace, be still.' And there was miraculous calm that came at that time. Father, as you know what we feel in our hearts today, we pray again that Jesus walking in our midst would say again, 'Peace, be still,' and that we might find that same peace and calm in our hearts in these moments. Let it be so, Lord Jesus, as only you can do it. We pray and ask these things in your name and for your glory. Amen."

I could feel the peace that Brother Bob referred to, but my emotions were still teetering back and forth. I tried to maintain my calm façade. Brother Bob continued, "'For now we see through a glass, darkly; but then face to face: now I know in part; but then shall I know...' 1 Corinthians 13:12 (KJV). I've read that verse many times. I've preached from this passage several times, but I guess there's never been a time when I've felt the truth of that more than right now. There are some things that we just don't fully understand. I don't have any easy answers. I don't have any deep theological or philosophical or psychological things to say. I have the same feelings in my heart that you have in your heart right now. I fight today to hold back the tears, just like you do. But I do have, in the midst of not being able to understand and in the midst of acknowledging that I know only in part, I do have faith. I do know that someday all of my questions are going to be answered, and my understanding will be enlightened. But right now, we look through a glass darkly, and we know only in part. We acknowledge that. We admit it without any shame. But there are three things that I want to share with you and to enlarge upon that I think God has placed in my heart and that I hope and pray will touch your heart in a special way."

As always, Brother Bob's calm reassurance gave me great comfort as he began the eulogy. "I first of all want to talk to you about some things that we will never ever regret. I guess to understand what I mean by that statement, I need to set it in contrast. We all regret from a human standpoint that Brad was not given a longer time upon this earth—that his time was so very brief. But none of us regret that we had him. We can regret that we had him for only three years but never regret those three years. Isaiah 11 (KJV) says, 'A little child shall lead them.' I think we could expand that into a lot of different things that would be true. Not only a little child shall lead them, but a little child shall teach them, a little child shall lift them, a little child shall bless them, a little child shall love them, a little child shall be loved by them, a little child shall be an enrichment to their lives. We had him with us for only three years, but we are better off for having had him even though it was for only those three years. And we will never regret what he taught us and what he brought us."

Then Brother Bob began to share some of the personal stories we had told him about our son. It was heartwarming to hear them, but as the reality of the moment hit me, I could feel myself making that noise again. It was like groaning spilling out of my heart. I tried to hold it in, but it was impossible. The medication made my responses slow, and my mind was muddled, but I knew I didn't want my family to see such raw emotion. No matter how hard I tried to stifle my sobs, they kept coming. The waves of emotion swept over me as Sam tried his best to comfort me in spite of his own pain. He wrapped his arms around me and said, "It's going to be okay, darlin'. We're gonna make it through this. I love you and Adam so much." I couldn't speak, but his words gave me the strength to recompose myself. Time seemed to stand still. I didn't want to let go of my son. The service seemed to take forever, but at the same time, I was afraid it would end too quickly. I didn't want to face what was next.

Brother Bob continued, "I asked Sam and Mona to just talk about Brad yesterday, and I was so blessed. As in the midst of tears and memories, the things that they remembered that he said and the things that they did as a family, I could talk a very long time about all of the things they remembered. His very happy spirit; his friendliness; his love for his family, and he didn't hesitate to say it; his singing "Jesus Loves Me;" his prayers; his being a helper; and so much more. When I think of all the things his parents and his family know about Brad, I know that they are thankful that Brad came their way and that they will never, never regret those three years that he was with them." How beautifully our pastor had expressed what was in our hearts. Tears continued to flow as memories flooded our minds.

Brother Bob began again, "Here is a second thing on my heart in a special way. Not only what we will never regret, but what we, in faith, can accept. Brad is with the Lord Jesus Christ. Our faith tells us that is true. There is a song we sing sometimes: "Safe in the Arms of Jesus." Those scriptures that I read about Jesus taking a child in His arms; about His drawing a lamb to his bosom—my faith tells me, and I can accept that on Wednesday night, Jesus took little Brad into His arms and drew him to his bosom. My faith tells me, also, that we will see him again with Jesus Christ. There is a story in the book of 2 Samuel about the death of a child and the father gave this testimony in that story, 'I cannot bring him back again, but I shall go to him.' I believe that. I believe that when someone is safe in the arms of Jesus, we will go to be with him in God's appointed time."

Our dear pastor said, "There are some things in faith that we can accept. Sam and Mona, God trusted you to care for Brad for these three years. You can trust Jesus to take care of him for you now. "But, there is a third thing on my heart that I want to share and that is what we never want to forget. Not only what we never will regret and what we can accept, but what we must never, never forget. Where there is love, there's going to be grief. You cannot keep that from happening. The deeper the love, the greater the grief. And that's why you feel so deeply. If you didn't love so much, you wouldn't feel the sadness you feel. So the very deep pain and hurt that you feel in your spirit today is a testimony of your deep love. I thank God for that."

He continued, "When I think of things we must never forget, I remember what the Bible says. God is our refuge and our strength. The Lord is our helper. That the Lord will never put on us more than we can bear. That nothing will separate us from the love of God. That His grace is always sufficient. I know that you are experiencing and will continue to experience that." I knew these words were true as I recalled what Cynthia had whispered in my ear the day after Brad's death. I could hear the sobs of people sitting around me as Brother Bob described the love of God. I couldn't help but wonder if they were crying for us or if they had been reminded that life is fleeting and everyone will face God some day.

My mind was drawn back to the service as I heard Brother Bob begin again. "When I think of the things we must never forget, I remember something the Bible tells us about families. It tells us about a very special family. We don't think about this too much unless we're forced to by circumstances. Paul's writing to the church in Ephesus said, 'I bow my knees unto the Father of our Lord Jesus Christ.' He says, I pray for you. And then he ads this, 'The Lord Jesus Christ for whom the whole family in heaven and earth is named.' Sometimes, part of our family can be in heaven and part of it can be on earth. Yet, as God evaluates everything, it's still one family. I hope you will never forget that. Little Brad had not reached that age of accountability where he had to seek Christ as his personal Savior. You see, every child, until he reaches that age, is safe in Jesus, and they're part of your family, still. Part are in heaven, and part are on earth." What a beautiful way to think of our family. Although we were separated by death, we were still a family.

As Brother Bob continued, I sensed a shift in his tone. Our prayer had been that others would be touched by Brad's memorial and that they would understand clearly how Sam and I trusted the Lord and looked to God for strength, even through a tragedy like this. "There is a fourth thing we should never forget. That is that, over and over, Christians are referred to as 'children of God.' You must receive the kingdom of God as a little child. You must be converted by becoming as little children with their childlike faith and childlike humility and their childlike trust. I hope that every one of us here today will take home with us the realization of the joy and pleasure that our children can be to us. Children show love, devotion, obedience, and that childlike faith and trust. As a child of God, this is what I should show to him. I should bring to him my childlike faith and my obedience and my love. I should place my arms around the Lord Jesus Christ and say, 'I love you.'

"If we walk in faith, sometimes that faith can be tried. The Bible speaks of childlike faith. Every experience can draw us closer to God. I already know by talking to Sam and Mona that they are saying in their hearts amidst their grief and sorrow, 'How can I be a better Christian through all of this? How can I serve you better, Lord, through all of this?' The Lord is going to show you the way and walk with you every step. You are going to continue to feel grief, but He will comfort you. You will continue to know only in part, but by faith you know that every question will be answered, by and by."

Brother Bob's voice broke, and tears flowed from his eyes as he said, "I just can't say in words how much we love you. But you know that. God bless each of you grandparents in a special way with the comfort you need at a time such as this. And know, as you leave this place in a few moments, that if you have Jesus Christ in your heart, you will again be able to face tomorrow."

As Brother Bob finished his remarks, our dear friend, Ron Henderson, sang the last song, "Because He Lives." The song says, "Because He lives, all fear is gone; Because I know He holds the future / And life is worth the living, Just because He lives!" These words expressed the hope that we would cling to in the days ahead. I didn't realize it at the time, but that day was St. Patrick's Day. It was also Ron's birthday. He sang the song beautifully as only he could.

As the service finally came to an end, the funeral directors led people to walk by and view the casket. Friends hugged us and whispered, "I'm so sorry for your loss," and "I'll be praying for you." Many said, "Please let me know if you need anything." We were grateful for their thoughts and prayers. It seemed to take forever for the stream of people to pass by, but eventually everyone but the family was gone, and we were left alone with our child. We had placed some of Brad's toys on the altar beside the casket. We spent several minutes viewing our son's body for the last time. Then, Sam and I leaned over his casket as I kissed his forehead and whispered, "I love my sweet baby." As we gradually accepted the fact that our time together had ended, we placed some of the toys he loved into the casket beside him. I remember how strange it seemed knowing that those things were no longer important to him. But it made me feel better knowing that he was surrounded by things he loved. Unfortunately, the things he loved most would be left behind.

The stream of cars left the church, with us leading the procession. Maple Grove Cemetery was only a few blocks away. As we drove in, I saw the customary green canopy flapping in the breeze. The tiny white casket was resting on two metal bars that were draped with fabric. We slowly approached the area where we were to be seated, and it occurred to me that the bars were there to help lower the casket into the ground. The flowers surrounding the casket looked so fresh and alive. Brother Bob began the graveside service by reading Scripture. I don't remember much except staring at the box that held my baby's remains. As Sam held my hand and placed his arm around my shoulders, I thanked God for his love.

The service was brief, and people gradually left. Most of them weren't aware that Brad wasn't buried that day. His body was placed in the hearse and driven immediately to the state medical examiner's office for the autopsy.

# REMEMBERING BRAD

Walking into our house after the funeral was difficult. The silence was deafening. Even with people all around us, there was a quiet acknowledgment that life would never be the same. People came and left; most didn't know what to say. Many just shed tears and gave us hugs, offering to help in any way they could. There were many attempts at explaining why God had allowed this to happen. Some said, "God needed another flower in heaven." Some said, "Brad was too good to live in this world." Some even said, "God took him to spare him from some worse fate on earth." They meant well, but trying to sum up the death of our child in such succinct terms made his life seem less significant. If there is anything that we desired, it was that Brad's life would have lasting meaning and significance. He only lived for three short years, but he did live, and his life touched others. He hadn't had time to build a legacy, but those who knew him remembered the love that he gave so freely to others. We didn't know why God had allowed his life to end so quickly, but we clung to Nahum 1:7 (KJV), "The Lord is good, a stronghold in the day of trouble, and He knoweth them that trust in him."

After experiencing such tragedy, our hearts were laid open for the world to see. Sam says we were bulletproof. We had suffered the greatest loss imaginable. But I wasn't prepared for the events that lay ahead. My mother's husband, Christie, was there for the funeral and stayed the night. He planned to go home the next day, but she would stay as long as possible. As he and I were sharing a quiet moment, I learned a family secret that had been kept from me for thirty-one years. I asked, "Is it possible that you could be my father?"

He just looked at me and said, "Go ask your mother." In my heart, I knew the answer. But my mind was racing as I walked into the next room and approached my mother.

She was ironing, and I just blurted out, "I asked Christie if he was my father, and he told me to come ask you."

She slowly looked up and said, "Yes, he is." I couldn't help but wonder if she was shocked by the question. But, judging from her reaction, she must have seen this coming.

"How could you have kept this from me for all these years?" I asked as tears began to fall.

She tried to explain, "In those days you didn't talk about things like that. Once I began covering up the truth, it was hard to go back and undo it." Memories of things she had told me as a child came flooding back… "If you ever tell a lie, then you have to tell another one to back it up. Pretty soon you forget what you've told."

It all made sense to me now. Her negative attitude toward men; her long relationship with a man who was already married; she had held onto the hope that he would marry her…because of me.

The man that I thought was only my mother's husband was actually my father. Needless to say, this turned my world upside down and added to the anxiety of the situation. The timing was terrible, and there were a lot of repercussions. I couldn't believe that I hadn't figured this out before now. I look a lot like Christie's sister, and I now realized how much I actually look like him. The conversation I had a week ago with my sister came to my mind, "Have you ever noticed how much you look like Mildred?" Tara had asked. Christie and I didn't discuss it much before he left the next day, but Mother and I talked about it at length in the days and weeks that followed. I wondered how this would change my relationship with Christie. I guess I secretly hoped he would finally be the father I had never had.

It's not uncommon for families to face hidden issues after a death. There's something about grief that brings those issues to the surface. When people's emotions lay bare, they feel they can't be hurt any deeper. I know that sounds strange, but it's almost like they realize the brevity of life and decide to make peace with the people they care about. The masks come off, and people are more real. It doesn't last long, but it is a miraculous thing to watch.

Sam and I returned to the cemetery a couple of days later to lay our son's body to rest. Our friends Ken and Karen Green accompanied us. We prayed together as we watched the workmen lower his body into that deep hole. Karen said, "Brad was so precious. I have some great memories of him." Many of the flowers were still there from the funeral and Ken took out his pocketknife, cut a red rose from one of the arrangements, and handed it to me. Sam held me in his arms as tears streamed down our faces, I whispered, "I love you, Brad." Then I dropped the rose into the hole, and I heard a soft thud as it landed on top of his tiny casket.

We went home, once again, trying to understand how this could have happened. Our children had been healthy. They were under the care of a pediatrician who had given them their shots on time and saw them for regular medical checkups. We were good parents. What could have happened to this apparently healthy child? The autopsy would hopefully provide some answers, but the results would not be known for at least two weeks.

People from church continued to come to our home for weeks. Friends would stop by and spend as much time as they could. They brought food for days. I had to watch Adam because he would eat nothing but donuts and cookies. Gradually, people went back to their normal routines, and one day Adam looked at me and said, "When are all the people coming?" He had become accustomed to the attention he received. I explained that they had to return to their own family responsibilities. Adam hadn't had much discipline lately, and it was showing. There were so many different people watching over him, he got by with murder. I knew the day was coming when I would have to confront his disobedience, but I was hoping Sam would do it. The thought of spanking him was unbearable. Adam was our only child, now, and he suddenly seemed all the more precious. I just didn't have the strength to deal with correcting him.

For everyone else, life goes on, and people gradually return to their own routines. To us, it seemed like the world had stopped turning. As everyone else went about their lives, it became increasingly clear that ours could never be the same. My mother stayed with us as long as she could to help me with the cooking, cleaning, and laundry. But eventually, even she had to return to her home in Arkansas. It was a sad day when she had to leave. Adam and I would miss her terribly.

There were so many unanswered questions. We struggled to accept what had happened and that we never even got to say good-bye. Doubts and fears took hold of us at times. How could we live on when our child had died? Parents are supposed to protect their children. I was a careful mother. I had been so conscientious about safety and protecting them from strangers. But ultimately, even I couldn't protect him from this. There must have been a health problem that we weren't aware of. There had to be an explanation.

At other times we bravely thanked God for the circumstances that surrounded Brad's death. It was almost as if God had sheltered us as much as possible. He had provided a doctor to administer CPR immediately. He had placed Sam at home just a few blocks away instead of out on a job. He had allowed it to happen in a place where we were immediately surrounded by love and support. I could have been at home alone with both boys when it happened. Thankfully, Brad didn't suffer, but rather he had died instantly. And I was thankful each time the last words that Brad spoke to me rang in my ears, "I love you, Mommy."

A couple of weeks after Brad's death, Sam suggested that we go to western Oklahoma for a few days. His family has acres of farmland with lots of fishing ponds. At first I resisted the idea because I didn't want to leave. It would be devastating to return to an empty house. But, I knew that Sam needed to get away. He loved to fish, and it would be an opportunity for him to clear his head and get some perspective. I didn't want any perspective. I just wanted to stay close to my son's memory.

We made the three-hour drive to stay with Sam's cousin Ronnie and his wife, Marilyn. They had two daughters, Ronna and Shanda, who sometimes babysat when I was there. They also had a son, Devin, who Adam loved to spend time with on the farm. We arrived on Friday afternoon, and that evening I was standing in the kitchen trying to help Marilyn cook. I was shocked when Marilyn answered the phone and handed it to me.

"It's for you, Mona."

I said, "Thanks," as I took the phone. I dreaded hearing the voice on the other end. It was Gus Shi.

He said, "Mona, the autopsy report is in." There was a knot in my stomach as he began to tell me the results. Gus said, "According to the state medical examiner, Brad had no broken bones or disease in his body. The only indication of injury was a small bruise on his chin where he fell." There was no explanation for why Brad had died. I couldn't believe what I was hearing. Gus said, "I'm sorry that there isn't a better explanation."

I could tell it was hard for him to give me that information, so I said, "Thank you for keeping me informed," and I hung up the phone.

I walked back into the kitchen and told Marilyn what Gus had said. I tried to carry on a normal conversation as I described the details, but Marilyn could see that I was struggling to maintain my composure. I could feel tears beginning to fall as she said, "Mona, why don't you go lie down on my bed and rest for a little while?" I gladly accepted her offer because I could feel myself falling apart as the realization of what had just happened began to sink in.

As I walked into Marilyn's bedroom, my mind was whirling with thoughts about what Gus had told me. How could this be true? Modern medical science couldn't tell me what had caused my son's death? I was conflicted over the lack of an explanation and at the same time relieved by the fact that there was nothing wrong with my son. It was almost as if God had just reached down and taken him without any explanation. As I lay there, I began to feel anxiety rising up in my heart. I cried out to God to give me an explanation for why Brad had died. I muttered through my tears, "You raised Lazarus from the dead! You healed people in the Bible! You raised Jairus's daughter from the dead! Why can't you tell me what happened to my son? Why can't you give me a vision right now? Write something on the wall in front of me, or roll out a movie screen and show me my son in heaven so that I'll know he's okay. Is that too much to ask?" As the words passed my lips, I felt God speak to my heart.

I want you to walk by faith, not by sight.

It wasn't an audible voice that I heard, but it might as well have been a booming voice over a megaphone. I was startled by the realization that God had answered my cries. He did care. I wept as I felt the heaviness of my heart lighten a bit. Once again, I was reminded of Scripture, and I felt the "peace that passes all understanding" take hold of my heart and my mind. I thanked God for answering my prayer, and then I slowly got up and rejoined the family. I still had to tell Sam the results of the autopsy and as I walked into the living room I saw that he and Ronny were watching TV.

I said, "Sam, can I talk to you for a minute?" He came toward me and we walked into a quiet room for some privacy. "Sam, Gus Shi just called."

"Well, what did he say?" Sam asked with expectancy.

"He said that the autopsy was back, and it showed no broken bones or disease in Brad's body."

Sam couldn't believe what he was hearing. He was as shocked as I had been. "Why can't medical science tell us what happened to our son? I just don't understand," he said.

Our minds whirled with the information we had been given. "Let's try to enjoy the weekend," he said. "We wouldn't feel any better if we were at home. I'll talk to Gus when we get back." So we tried not to let it dominate our thoughts, but we both felt a heaviness in our hearts.

After spending the weekend with Sam's family, we had to head back home. I could feel the sense of fear and dread rising in my spirit the closer we got. Finally we arrived and turned the key to open the back door. The three of us walked into our quiet house, and everything was just as we had left it. Once again, we had to accept the reality that Bradley was gone, and he would never, ever be back.

A few days after we returned, I received a call from the state medical examiner himself. He explained the results of the autopsy to me. He said, "I wish I could tell you exactly what caused your son's death, but I can only give you my best guess. There was no disease and no broken bones in Bradley's body, but the bruise on his chin indicates that he landed there when he fell. It's like a boxer's punch to the chin, and there have been incidents where a blow to that area of the chin could cause instant death. There is no way to know for sure."

After he explained a bit more, he said, "I'm very sorry for your loss." I could tell it was difficult for this man to give me this information. I didn't know what he looked like or what kind of person he was, but I could sense the sadness in his voice. I wondered if he had children of his own as I thanked him for calling.

Sam and I discussed the results, and we both concluded that regardless of the bruise on Brad's chin, he was dead before he hit the ground. The ladies in the nursery who saw him fall said that he fell "like a board." He never tried to catch himself, which indicates that he had lost consciousness before the fall. We may never know what caused Brad's death, but we know that God allowed it. This, like everything else in a Christian's life, is sifted through the hands of God.

I wanted to know if Bradley had suffered before he died. I asked Gus about this, and he assured me that Brad was dead instantly, and he did not suffer. Our conclusion that he was dead before he fell validates that as well. Thank God that my son never knew any pain. If this had to happen, at least God in his mercy chose not to allow him to suffer.

Burying a child was so hard. The funeral had to sum up his short life in the span of an hour. The songs had to reflect what we were feeling, and the headstone would represent the only legacy most people would ever know. The words would be etched in stone—forever. It's so permanent, and you don't get a second chance. As his mother, I felt responsible for preserving his memory. How do you sum up a child's life on a cold slab of granite? What about their dreams and yours? How is it possible to tell their life's story without sharing the details? Maybe I should just stand at the cemetery and explain it to people as they pass by. *His life mattered. He was loved. He has a brother who has lost so much, and he's only five years old. His father has a broken heart.*

One of my greatest fears was that I would forget my memories of Brad. There were so many precious times we had spent together as a family. The very morning of his death is etched into my mind. Adam was at kindergarten, and Sam had already left for work. I was sitting in my office, still in my pajamas with no makeup on, and my hair wasn't combed. I heard Brad get up and head to the bathroom. As he caught my eye, he said, "Good morning, Mother."

I said, "Good morning, darling. I love you."

He said, "I love you too."

Then I heard the unmistakable sound of the toilet lid as he threw it back with a *clank*. Next came the sound of a mighty rushing fountain as he unleashed the morning flood—I was just glad he made it! I smiled to myself as I met him in the hallway. Kneeling down to greet him, I felt a warm little body as he reached up to put his arms around me for a hug. He had that morning smell that only children have and mothers never forget. I picked him up, carried him into his room, and playfully tossed him onto the bed. I leaned over the bed to give him a tickle and said, "I look terrible this morning."

As I did, he reached up, put his hand on my cheek, and said, "You're pretty, Mommy." Moments like that melt a mother's heart.

We got dressed to go pick Adam up at school. I dressed Brad in his black Mickey Mouse sweatshirt and black sweatpants. We picked Adam up at kindergarten, and on the way home I asked them if they wanted to go to McDonald's grand opening for lunch. Brad said, "We goin' to Backdonald's, Adam. Backdonald's!" I had Adam call Sam at the office and ask, "Dad will you come to McDonald's with us? *Please*? It's the first day they're open!"

Sam said, "I sure will! I don't want to miss takin' my little buddies to the grand opening." The boys were so excited! Ronald McDonald and all his friends were there, and they were passing out balloons. Brad kept asking the characters for another balloon, and he had several before we left. While we were eating, we saw some friends from church. Little did we know that one of them would witness our son's fall in a few short hours.

There are unique things about each child, like certain mannerisms and phrases. Many of these quickly fade from memory if they aren't written down or videotaped. Although I had lots of videos of my children, I still felt a need to document my memories of Brad in some way. There were days when I couldn't concentrate on anything else. Finally, a poem came to me. It felt so good to write down the things that I treasured most. It was my way of clinging to his memory.

I've heard it said that a life is summed up in the *dash* between the date of birth and the date of death. Bradley barely had a dash, because he only lived three short years. It took months for me to choose a headstone for Brad's grave, but once it was chosen, we had the poem I had written inscribed on the back.

# IN MEMORY OF BRADLEY EDWARD ADKISSON

## FEBRUARY 10, 1986-MARCH 15, 1989

Loving memories of happy days,
Little boys' laughter and charming ways.
Two toy bikes...two baseball bats,
Torn tee shirts and old army hats.
A knock at the door, Brad peeks through the curtain.
He thinks it's Dad, but he looks to make certain.
"Dad's home! Dad's home!" as he opens the door.
"How's my partner?" Dad sweeps him from the floor.
Suspended in air by a big sturdy arm,
Dad will keep him safe from harm.
Tangled fishing line and minnows in a pail,
Nothing for supper but another fishing tale.
Time for bed and prayers on our knees,
A special time that only God sees.
One is almost six, the other just turned three.
A home filled with love, as happy as can be.
Big hugs for Mom, and wrestling with Dad.
The things that bring joy to Adam and Brad.
"Mom, help me learn to count by twos."
"My piggies are cold. Get my Mickey Mouse shoes."
An icy dagger pierces my breast,
Reality is back, an unwelcome guest.
Now there are three instead of four,
Nothing is the same as it was before.
All our souls to the core were shaken,
When our little boy's last breath was taken.

By sudden death, that mysterious chill.
But God whispered softly, "Peace, be still.
Let the Father of mercies and God of all comfort
Comfort you that you might comfort others.
The time will come from your mourning to rest,
Because you have Adam, you must do your best."
Then one day, I began to realize,
As I looked at this through the Father's eyes.
We're still a family of four, full of love.
There are three of us here and one up above.

Mother

# SWEET SURRENDER

Marriage was designed by God to be a unique relationship between a man and woman. That relationship offers the opportunity for intimacy like no other relationship on earth. Unfortunately, I had not seen a good example of the marriage relationship from my parents. But as I grew in my relationship to God through the years, I learned to trust my husband more. Through Bible study, I had begun to grasp the purpose for marriage and the roles God intended for husbands and wives. Amazingly, as I learned to live out that role, respect for my husband grew as well. When we follow God's plan, the marriage relationship works together beautifully.

The home is supposed to be a sanctuary from the world and its battles. There are ways to make each family member feel loved and accepted at home. Things like greeting one another with a smile and a hug mean so much after a hard day's work. Or telling your children you're proud of them, even when they've had a disappointment. The home can be a wonderful buffer from the harshness of the world around us. Our home had grown into that kind of place. We still had disagreements, and none of us were all that God wanted us to be, but we were growing and learning to depend on him more and more. Our children were deeply loved and cared for, and they saw two parents who loved each other.

There is nothing that can prepare a marriage for the devastation brought from the loss of a child. I remember thinking, *This will either bring us closer together, or it will tear us apart.* Little did I know how true those words were. People were at our house day and night for weeks. They tried very hard to be considerate of our need for privacy, but at times, we had to escape to our bedroom to be alone.

The day after Brad's death, Sam and I were so exhausted from grief. It took every ounce of strength we could muster just to get through the day and do all of the things that had to be done. People helped us as much as they could, but there were certain things that only we could do. At one point during the day, we escaped to our bedroom to try to rest. Words were unnecessary because we could read each other's broken hearts. That brokenness made us extremely vulnerable. I've never felt such a strange yet comfortable feeling as I did that day. There were no defense mechanisms at work, only total transparency. Through the loss of our son, we shared a bond that few people have experienced. As we embraced, our bodies seemed to melt together. That was the closest I had ever felt to another human being. I remember thinking that this must be what God meant when he said that husband and wife were to become one flesh. The bond that was created from that experience still exists today.

They say that time heals all wounds, but how much time is the question. We struggled to maintain our sanity for months. Sam stayed as busy as possible, and I focused on Adam. One of the weirdest things about the grief process was the effect it had on my ability to function. I couldn't concentrate. I would try so hard to focus my mind on something, but it was impossible. I still have gaps in my memory of those days. Often I ask people to tell me what they remember, because I can't.

The things that I do remember are permanently imprinted on my mind. One such memory occurred during an evening after Adam was in bed. Sam and I were sitting on the couch in the living room. As our thoughts turned toward our memories of Brad, I began to cry. Often tears helped me release pent-up emotions that had to escape, or I would explode. I looked over at Sam, and his face was contorted, but there were no tears coming down. I asked him, "Why aren't you crying?" His voice cracked as he said, "I don't know how." We hugged one another tightly and just rocked back and forth. Gradually I began to hear the sobs that had been welling up in my husband for such a long time. It was like a dam had burst as the hurt and sadness were finally released.

I've read that sometimes men are afraid to cry because they fear being out of control. It's almost as if they're afraid if they start, they won't be able to stop. Sam had been taught to "hold your head up if it kills you." It wasn't considered manly to show emotion, but even the strongest of men could not bear the load he had been carrying. I think all of the pain from his father's death and dealing with his mother's loss had worn him down. And now, this loss was enough to break any man. But, in his typical fashion, Sam looked at me and said, "We can get through this—as long as I have you and Adam. The Lord will see us through." It was just not in his nature to stay down. Sam has always been an optimist, and again, he chose to look for something positive to cling to. Romans 8:28 (NIV) says, "And we know that in all things God works for the good of those who love him, who have been called according to his purpose." Sam often said, "God has allowed this for a reason. I just wish I knew what that reason was."

Understandably, we struggled to comprehend God's purpose and plan. One day we would be up, and then out of the blue something would happen to bring us down. In those times of doubt, Sam often said, "I wonder what God is trying to tell me from this experience. What have I done that caused God to punish me?" Fortunately, when those struggles were hardest for him, I was usually able to be strong. I would reassure him that God is a God of love and of mercy. Often a scripture would come to mind that offered hope. Words like Jeremiah 29:11 (NIV) that says, "For I know the plans I have for you, plans to prosper you and not to harm you, plans to give you hope and a future." It was as if God knew we couldn't both afford to be down. When my times of doubt and fear came, Sam was always there to reassure me of God's love and care for our family as well.

Many times I've seen a certain look on Sam's face, and I just know what he is thinking. He's usually thinking about a time he shared with our children, and then inevitably, the feeling of loss sinks in. Many times when we are talking to people, I begin to share about our loss. Sam's face often takes on a stern look of discomfort. It is still very difficult for him to talk about it. As the years have gone by, he has become more willing to share our story but not without a great deal of pain.

How could he think of our son Brad without remembering the times he had wrestled with him or put him to bed and tucked him in? How could he forget the feeling of those tiny arms around his neck? How could he not feel heartbroken when he put Adam to bed in a room that contained two bunk beds? Those wonderful memories haunted us as they were contrasted by the present reality.

It isn't just time that heals wounds. It's what you do during that time. Seeing Adam struggle to have Christmas made us realize how much we had to live for.

# SAY IT AGAIN, SAM

Nothing can prepare you for the impact that the loss of a child has on a family, especially its impact on a marriage. People have said to me, "Well, at least you have each other." But what they don't realize is that many times, you can't even be there for each other. Grief is a very personal experience. Sam and I grieved in very different ways. I remember reading in one of Billy Graham's books that 70 percent of marriages break up after losing a child. As I read those words, my heart sank. The very thought of losing my husband too was more than I could bear.

I read voraciously during those days. Books seemed to be a comfort to me. Their words helped me to process what was happening. Maybe that gave me some sense of control. I read a lot about the grief process and its different stages. Let's face it; this is not a topic people choose to read about unless they are forced to. I was desperate for information that would help us survive. With all of the baggage I had from my family, I knew that I wasn't equipped to deal with the emotionally charged issues we had to face. There were several books that really helped me cope. The first one was *Don't Take My Grief Away From Me* by Doug Manning. It helped me to realize that what I was feeling was normal, and there was no need to rush through the grief process. Another book I read was *Death and the Life After* by Billy Graham. Dr. Graham's writings are laced with Scripture and always point us to Christ as the answer to all our needs. It also talked about different kinds of losses, including the death of a child, and it directed me to Scripture passages that pertained to children. We took great comfort in those passages. God's Word soothes and brings healing in a way that nothing else on this earth can. Sometimes it felt like God was talking directly to me.

The book that I relied on most of all was the Bible. The words in 2 Corinthians 1:3-4 (NASB) were especially meaningful:

> Blessed be the God and Father of our Lord Jesus Christ, the Father of mercies and God of all comfort, who comforts us in all our affliction so that we will be able to comfort those who are in any affliction with the comfort with which we ourselves are comforted by God.

It gave me hope to think that my suffering might someday be used to help others. The worst thing I could imagine would be for my son's death to have no lasting significance. His life was precious to me, and it was precious to God. If God could use me to help bring comfort to others, then I would feel blessed.

Sam often heard me tell people about the events surrounding Brad's death. That's the way I worked through the grief process. But that isn't the way he dealt with it. He would occasionally tell me that he didn't want to talk about it, and he didn't know why

I had to keep bringing it up with people. I tried to be considerate, but what had happened to us had become such a big part of our life, it was unavoidable. We lived in a small town, and that event affected a lot of people. Even people we didn't know were touched by our tragedy. We still to this day run into people who recognize us, and we have no idea who they are. It seemed to me that people needed to hear us talk about it. I think it put them more at ease because they didn't know whether to mention it or not. The way I learned to deal with it was to bring it up first so they wouldn't have to struggle with a way to broach the subject.

I was blessed to have friends who would let me relive the story over and over. But men don't usually approach grief that way. They tend to avoid the emotional discussions, and they sure don't want to relive the horrible events, blow by blow. Rather than talking about it, Sam turned to the two methods he had relied on for years: work and fishing.

Work offered an opportunity for Sam to refocus. We obviously had to have an income, so throwing himself into his work was justifiable. This may have been when God taught him to be faithful and to persevere. Diligence, or faithfulness, and perseverance are fruits of the Spirit that Sam has relied upon heavily through the years, and they have served him well. I've learned so much from watching him seek God's will and direction for our family and for his businesses. It never ceases to amaze me at how God answers the prayers of his people.

Sam fished as often as he could. Sometimes he would take someone with him, and sometimes he would go alone. He really enjoyed farm ponds that were close to home. He would usually fish until dark and come in with a mess of fish to clean. There is nothing he loves more than fresh fish.

We used to take our boys fishing occasionally. Adam would run around on the bank, and Brad would catch the minnows in the pail. Sam never got much fishing done when they went along, but we made some great memories. I'm sure, in the solitude of moments spent fishing alone, Sam reminisced about those times. Memories for us have become like still-life paintings in the back of our minds. We never want to forget a single one, and we are haunted by the paintings that were left unfinished.

Through the years, Sam has learned to be more vocal about his feelings. Like most people who survive a tragedy, we read one another's thoughts and mannerisms pretty well. I can usually tell when he is uncomfortable talking, and I've learned to wait until we are alone to ask what he was thinking about. He has learned to read me as well. We will never escape the pain of what has happened to our family, but I guess you could say we've learned to cope. I still talk, and Sam still fishes, but we've learned to honor each other's needs.

# DON'T TELL ME THAT

One of the most difficult things to understand after a tragedy is how other people react to you. I could sense the discomfort some people felt just being around me. It really caught me off guard at first. As I read more about the grief process, I began to understand that most people are unprepared for such an experience, just as I was. There isn't a class offered at church about how to treat people who have lost a loved one. And we sure don't learn it in school. So most people fumble for words or avoid you all together.

I'll never forget the first time I realized how difficult it could be for someone to see me after Brad's death. I was at the post office, and as I was making my way up the steps, I saw a lady I knew from church. Instead of acknowledging me or stopping to talk, she acted like she didn't see me and hurried back to her car. I know she saw me, and I couldn't imagine why she wouldn't want to speak to me. I didn't know of anything I had done to offend her. But it suddenly dawned on me that she probably didn't know what to say. It still hurt a little, but it made me sensitive to other people's feelings of discomfort.

How do you say hello to someone and act normally when you know their world has fallen apart? Some people are afraid they'll make me cry or make me sad. What they don't realize is that, yes, it will make me sad to talk about the death of my child, but more than that, it makes me feel good that someone else remembers him. People react to grief differently, so it's best to simply state, "I don't know what to say, but I'm sorry for the loss." You can usually tell pretty quickly by how the grieving person reacts to that statement whether you should continue to discuss it or simply move on.

Sometimes, I got the opposite reaction. People would talk to me and start crying or tell me why God had allowed this to happen. Usually it was because "God needed another little angel" or "Maybe God knew that Brad would have rejected the Lord in the future, so God took him on home." Believe me, there is no comfort in thinking that the God of love and mercy I know would use such shallow reasons for taking my son. Often I would end up comforting others and assuring them that I was trusting God, whatever the reason for my son's death might have been. I have come to terms with the fact that I'll never know *why* this side of heaven—so I don't ask.

That is why I often looked for opportunities to share my story with people. Many times I would be asked how many children I had, and I learned to tell people that I had two, "My oldest son is Adam, and my son Brad is in heaven." People were usually either shocked or inquisitive. I always prayed for an opportunity to share the hope that I have of seeing my son again someday. Sometimes it would lead to lengthy discussions about God, and sometimes it wouldn't. But it always pointed people to Christ.

For the most part, people made an attempt to acknowledge what had happened to us, and Sam and I learned to appreciate their efforts. I became accustomed to putting people at ease right away so it would no longer be an issue. I'm very comfortable talking about my children, and sometimes that takes people by surprise. But what could be more natural for a mother than to talk about her children? Just because they aren't here physically doesn't mean they aren't part of our family. People were usually surprised, if not shocked. Then I would take the opportunity to tell them how good God has been to us through our tragedy. It seemed that most people were encouraged by my story. I guess they figured if I could make it through that, then there was hope for them in their circumstances. I always tried to point people to Christ because it is only by faith in Him that I'm able to make it through.

In May, after Brad's death in March, my sister called to tell me that she was pregnant. I know it was difficult for her to make that phone call. The last thing she wanted to do was add to my sadness. I was very happy for her, but it did remind me of how much I had lost, and it was ironic that she had probably conceived around the time of Brad's death. I didn't know it at the time, but Tara's daughter, Hollie—who was ten months younger than Brad—had been waking up at night with nightmares. She would cry and ask, "Why can't I go to McDonald's with Brad? I just want to play with him!" She and Brad had been very close, and she was too young to understand what had happened. This went on for months until she finally became accustomed to his absence.

I was very blessed to have a few close friends who spent time with me and didn't mind me telling about the events surrounding Brad's death repeatedly. I can remember sitting in a pizza place at lunch and reliving every detail for the twentieth time. My dear friends Paula and Cynthia endured many hours of listening to me tell the story over and over again. We had known each other since Adam was a baby, and the three of us each had a son the same age. We had all been through difficult times over the years; Paula had lost both of her parents by the time she was a teenager. She lost her mother to breast cancer, and her father had committed suicide. Cynthia had two children at that time, who were born with SCIDS (Severe Combined Immune Deficiency Syndrome), which means they lacked the ability to make T cells that provide immunity from disease. Her first son, Matthew, had almost died before he had a bone marrow transplant. I thank God for their prayers and support through losing my son. As I recalled the incidents time and time again, I think it helped me to process what had happened.

Sudden death is very difficult to accept. It takes time to work through the grief process and come to terms with what actually took place. It's not like a loss from long-term illness where you see a loved one suffer and can at least find some relief in their departure from pain. When someone dies suddenly, you don't even get to say good-bye. I've often compared it to an amputee. The difference is that no one can tell when part of your heart has been amputated.

# A RAY OF HOPE

Brad's death occurred on March 15th. My mother's birthday was April 2nd; mine was April 16th; and Adam's was May 2nd. We also had Easter and Mother's Day in there somewhere, then came Memorial Day and Father's Day in June. The firsts always seem to be the hardest. We faced one after another, but we made it through each one by relying on God's mercy and grace. Friends were good about sending us cards and dropping by to check on us occasionally. We stayed active in church and were there the very next day after the funeral. It felt good to be with people who cared about us.

I was adamant that I wanted another child. Sam and I each had only one sibling. My family was fractured, and I didn't grow up with close relationships. Sam grew up with lots of cousins and extended family who got together every Christmas at their grandmother's house. Sam also spent summers on the family farm in western Oklahoma, where he had lots of time with aunts and uncles and cousins. It sounded like so much fun when he described it to me. He had many stories about riding horses with his cousins and learning to drive a tractor.

I had never experienced anything like that, and I wanted Adam to have at least one more sibling to grow up with. I couldn't bear the thought of him being lonely. Sam and I talked about it, but he wasn't crazy about the idea. He wanted to wait and give it some time. I knew my biological clock was ticking and didn't think we should wait. Adam was already six years old, and they would be so far apart.

We always went to Arkansas for the Fourth of July. We would stay with my sister, Tara, and her husband, Roger, and have a big celebration. Christie's birthday was on the Fourth of July, and he always joked that *everybody* celebrates his birthday. That July, after Brad's death in March, we loaded Adam up and made the annual trip. This year would be so different. It had been less than four months since we lost Brad, and it was hard to leave because we dreaded returning home.

This would be the first time I had seen Christie since I found out he was my father. Adding to the stress was the secret hope in my heart that he would welcome me with open arms and hug me and tell me how thankful he was that I was his daughter.

We did our best to make things as normal as possible for Adam. Roger had a camper set up behind their house, and Tara insisted that we stay out there so we would have more privacy. Adam slept in the house with the other kids.

It had become obvious to me that since Sam was resistant to the idea of having another child, I was going to have to resort to more calculated means. I knew he would be happy once I was pregnant. He finally succumbed to my charms, and I was pretty sure that I had conceived that weekend.

About a month later, I had a pregnancy test, and it was positive. Sam's thirty-fifth birthday was August

22, and as our little family of three was gathered around the table, I gave him a birthday card that read, "Congratulations, you're going to be a daddy again." We were all ecstatic! It felt so good to have something to celebrate. Of course, we called the relatives and told them the good news. You could hear the joy in their voices and just a touch of sadness—or fear.

We decided to tell our friends at church that I was expecting. The news was just too good, and we couldn't contain it any longer! On that Wednesday evening we were gathered for dinner in the Fellowship Hall; the very room where Brad had died. Brother Bob said, "Church family, please listen. Sam and Mona have something to tell us."

Sam stepped to the microphone and said, "I have some great news to share. We are expecting a baby!"

You should have heard the yelling and applause! People were so happy to hear the good news. After watching us go through such a terrible loss, they were thrilled to be able to celebrate with us.

My pregnancy progressed without many complications. I had some morning sickness early on, but it had subsided by the third or fourth month. I seemed to get big a lot quicker this time! My body definitely remembered how to expand. I didn't look too bad from the back, but when I turned to the side, my belly stuck straight out! People always said that's how you look when you're carrying a boy. I wasn't so sure about that, but Sam and I definitely wanted to know the sex of the baby this time. It was more practical at this point to be well prepared. We had experienced enough surprises for a lifetime. So I had an ultrasound to check the sex of the baby, and they assured me that it was another boy. Sam was ecstatic. I would have been delighted to have a little girl, but I had grown to have a very special place in my heart for little boys. Adam was thrilled at the prospect of another little brother.

We knew this child would never replace Brad. He would always hold a special place in our hearts that no one else could ever fill. But the new baby gave us hope for the future; hope that life could somehow be normal again, and we could at least move forward. I began turning the bedroom that I had been using as an office into a nursery. It was right next to my room, and it would be easier to hear the baby when he cried. Adam had always shared a room with Brad, but he had it all to himself now. I gradually packed away the toys that were too young for Adam to play with and slowly tried to remove Brad's things. It was so hard to change things without knowing how Adam would react. Did he find comfort in some of those toys? Would his room feel cold without his brother's familiar belongings? I tried to get a feel for his preferences as we slowly adapted to our new way of life.

One sad moment came when I was putting away some of the bedding that was on Brad's lower bunk. Adam seemed disturbed, so I asked him, "Honey, are you sad that I'm putting away Brad's things? I can leave them out if it makes you feel better."

Adam looked down at the blue blanket on Brad's bed and said, "I've always wanted that blanket. Can I sleep with it now?"

Big tears welled up in his eyes, and I grabbed him and held him close. "Of course you can, sweetheart! I'm sure Brad would want you to have his blanket."

We sat and talked about how sad it was that Brad was no longer with us. I told Adam, "I'm so glad that I still have you. Your dad and I love you so much, and we thank God for you every day." Adam slept with that blue blanket for many years.

I often mentioned Brad, and I knew it was important that I encourage Adam to talk about him. One day as I was folding clothes, Adam said to me, "Sometimes I feel sad because I let Brad get into trouble for stuff I did."

I said, "Oh, honey, I'm so sorry that you feel sad, but the reason you feel sad is because you know what you did was wrong. Brad loved you very much, and I know that he knew how much you loved him. Sometimes brothers mistreat one another, but that doesn't mean you don't love each other. It's important that you pray and ask God to forgive you for not telling the truth."

I could feel the sense of relief Adam felt when he unloaded the burden of guilt he had been carrying. I could only imagine what Brad would have done if he had been there. I think he would have grabbed Adam and hugged him and told him, "It's okay, Bubba." Tears come to my eyes even now as I remember the tender love between my two precious little boys.

That fall, my mother had come to visit and help me get the nursery ready. We were busy doing something in the kitchen, and Adam was playing in the living room. He liked to take the cushions off the sofa and use them to make a tent. I guess he hadn't done this since Brad's death, because that day he found Brad's Sippy cup stashed under the sofa where they used to play. Moments like this would always bring back memories. He would reminisce about what he and Brad used to do together, and then we would laugh through our tears. Well, Mother and I did most of the crying. Adam was usually off on another adventure.

I wasn't prepared for the sadness that struck me during that first Christmas season after Brad's death. I would normally be decorating the house and buying presents, but that year I could hardly force myself to get the tree down from the attic. Adam was excited about Christmas, so we tried to go through the motions, even though our hearts were not in it. I remember sitting on the couch, and Sam was sitting in his recliner as Adam hung ornaments on the tree. Neither of us could bring ourselves to help him. Adam would say, "Come on, Mom. Help me decorate the tree." He would take me by the hand and try to pull me up. I couldn't stand to see him suffer another loss, so I tried to help him hang the ornaments. There is simply no way for us adults to follow those familiar traditions and act like everything is the same. Of course it isn't. It is impossible for things to be as they once were, but what do you do instead?

In my heart, I felt so bad for celebrating Christmas while my son was lying in a cold grave. How could any mother be happy when she knew one of her children was dead? It didn't seem right for me to be alive and breathing, yet I knew I had to go on because of Adam. He had been through enough. He didn't deserve to have his parents check out on him too.

Christmas is for celebrating the birth of Christ, but it is a magical event for children, and I wanted Adam to experience as much magic as we could manage to give him. We made it through that first Christmas by focusing on the one child we had left and the baby that I was carrying. It helped to remember that God understood. After all, he had lost a son too.

After Christmas, my sister gave birth to her second baby girl, Madalyn Michelle Beckham, and Adam and I went to Arkansas to see them in the hospital. Then in February we faced what would have been Brad's fourth birthday. It was devastating to think that he wouldn't be able to celebrate it with us. The flood of sadness and grief was—once again—overpowering. I felt I had to honor my son on his birthday, even though he wasn't here with us. So I baked a cake, and we had a little birthday celebration. We cried and told stories about him. We knew he was in heaven, but in our humanness, we missed his presence.

I tried to make sure Adam felt just as special as the brother he had lost. I had been counseled that children his age would accept the death and deal with it the way he saw his parents deal with it. So we tried to talk openly about it and not make him afraid to mention what had happened. We were as honest as we could be about our feelings, but we tried to focus on the great memories we had as a family. I feared that Adam would feel neglected or not as special as his brother. As we celebrated I said, "Adam, God has a special plan for your life. God's plan for Brad was to be in heaven, but God's plan for you is to be here with your dad and me and we're so glad that we have you."

Adam replied, "I'm so glad to be here with you and Dad too."

We continued to talk about our memories of Brad and share stories. I think it made us feel like he was still a part of our family and we would never forget him. It was important for Adam to see how much we loved Brad, even though he was no longer with us, because I instinctively knew that Adam would naturally wonder how we would feel if it had been him that was missing.

After Brad's birthday in February came the month of March, and the first anniversary of Brad's death. Christmas was tough, but for some reason, this was even tougher. A great sadness seemed to settle in my spirit. I don't know what it is about that milestone that makes it so difficult. Of course, it brings back the events of that day and the trauma of it all. Those events changed our lives forever. I had no experience with the first anniversary of a death, so it really caught me off guard. Learning how to manage your life and manage your grief at the same time seems impossible. Fortunately, every time I took one step of faith toward God, He took two steps toward me. I read Scripture constantly as well as every book about grief and death that I could find.

At the same time, I was struggling with my own identity. I had found out the day we buried my son that Christie was my real father, and it felt like my branch had been broken off the family tree. I needed to graft it onto the correct one in order to feel that I belonged. Unfortunately, Christie refused to acknowledge any mistakes from the past and would hardly discuss what had happened. So I was left to deal with those issues the best way I could. My mother and I actually went to some classes at a university about healing family wounds. She and I worked through much of what had happened and why. I was thankful for that. It took years for me to recover from the fact that my own father didn't want to claim me.

There were countless nights when Sam and I would be lying in bed talking, and something would trigger a memory of the hurt and abandonment I felt as a child. I would lie weeping in my husband's arms until I fell asleep. Sam would often say, "Any man who wouldn't claim you as his daughter had to be crazy. I would be proud to have you as my daughter. I feel sorry for him because he is the one who missed out on the blessings you would have brought into his life." That made me feel so much better for the moment, but the deep wound in my heart still felt like an open sore. It never seemed to heal.

I often searched the Scriptures for words of comfort. Once, I came upon Psalm 68:5 (NIV) that says that God is "father to the fatherless." Those words were refreshment to my soul. Though it took many years to resolve the hurt I felt, I developed a deep dependence upon God, the Father. As Romans 8:28 (NKJV) says, "And we know that all things work together for good to those who love God, to those who are the called according to His purpose." I'm counting on that.

# CHASING DREAMS

S am, Adam, and I labored over what name we would give the new baby. I was partial to family names and suggested we use Nathaniel because that was Sam's grandfather's name. Adam had been named after Sam's father, and Bradley's middle name was Edward, after my father. Finally Adam came up with the name Chase. It was perfect! We would name him Nathaniel Chase Adkisson. Sam's grandfather's initials were N.C., and so were his uncle's. My thirst for a family tradition was quenched, and we could call him by his middle name, which Adam thought was cool. I truly thought my son was a genius! How many six-year-olds do you know who could come up with a name for his baby brother? Years later I discovered that he had heard it on the Disney Channel. Some rock group had a singer named Chase. Oh, well.

My pregnancy progressed well until around the eighth month. I was having weekly doctor's visits by then, and the baby hadn't dropped. The doctor suggested that we should turn the baby. That didn't sound like much fun! They gave me an antihistamine to relax me, and as I lay on my back, the doctor took his hands and arms and rotated the baby in my womb. They monitored him with the ultrasound to make sure he wasn't in distress. It wasn't terribly painful, just very uncomfortable.

Adam had begun playing little league baseball, so I was at the ball field a lot that spring. I can remember sitting in the car watching a game when I felt Chase flip back around in my stomach. Oops! He would *stretch* his body from one of my ribs to the other. Then I would feel a foot gouging me in the side. It felt like he was going to poke a hole in my skin at times. When I went back to the doctor, he said we would just wait to see if he turned back around. I think he might have done a few somersaults, but he never did drop.

I went two weeks past my due date in April, and Dr. Trotter was headed out of town for a conference. He decided to schedule me to be induced on May 2, so he would be there for the delivery. I think he knew how nerve wracking it would be after all we had been though, and this was his way of comforting us the best way he could. He had been my doctor for years, and we trusted him.

Adam was delighted to hear that his new baby brother would be born on his seventh birthday! We let him stay home from school that day and be with us as we went to the hospital. My mother had come up to help out, and I had her take a picture of the three—I mean four—of us before we left for the hospital. I was definitely big enough to count as two. I felt like I was going to pop!

When we got to the hospital, they put me on a pitocin drip to induce labor. I had been given the same drug with each of my pregnancies to help speed up my labor. But this time was different. I went from a zero to birth in about eight hours. When I dilated to a six or seven, I asked for an epidural. I had never had one before, but I just couldn't take the pain this time. Sam and I were both afraid that something would go wrong. After losing a child, the possibility becomes so much more real.

Sam had coached me through the other two pregnancies, and he was right there with me again. Things had really changed in the delivery room since the last time I had a baby. They were much more lax about letting people come in. Several family members were in the waiting area and would take turns coming in to check on me. Mother brought Adam in early on, but by the time the labor got intense, I didn't want anybody but Sam.

Finally it came time to push. The epidural had kicked in, and I couldn't feel much. I looked over at Sam, but he wasn't there. My eyes scanned the room, and I found him standing, facing the wall. He was obviously distressed. I don't think he could stand to watch this time. I'm not sure if he feared the baby would be dead or if he thought something could happen to me. I kept pushing, and before I knew it, it was all over. I could hear the sounds of the baby as they prepped him, and then he joined me in a good cry. I think everybody was crying. Sam was standing beside me when they laid Chase on my chest. He said, "We did it again, darlin'! The baby is fine. I'm so proud of you!" I was tired and very relieved that both Sam and the baby were okay. All we needed now were his APGAR scores and to count his fingers and toes.

Sam wrapped him in his paper blanket, and he and the nurse took him to the nursery to be cleaned up. The scores were fine, and he was perfect—seven pounds, seven ounces—just like Sam and Adam and Brad. My mother told me that this time Sam came running into the waiting area and jumped over a barrier cord as he yelled, "We got another boy, and he weighs seven pounds, seven ounces!" Adam ran to him, and they hugged and gave each other high fives!

After a couple of days, we brought our baby home and began our new life together. I took Chase to the pediatrician for regular check-ups, and Dr. Mohan assured me that he was just fine. He was well aware of my concerns because he had been Adam and Brad's pediatrician as well.

When Chase was about three months old, I was changing his diaper, and I noticed that his right leg was discolored. When I held his feet over his head, part of his thigh would turn almost white and part of it was darker pink. It alarmed me because I had never noticed this before. I was afraid it was a circulatory problem. I called Dr. Mohan, and he had me bring him in to be checked. He felt sure that it was a kind of birthmark but wanted to be extra cautious considering our history. He called Children's Hospital in Oklahoma City that day and got us in that afternoon. By that time, I was terrified that something was wrong. I called Sam and told him, "I don't know what's wrong with Chase's leg. It could be something wrong with the circulation in that area. Dr. Mohan is sending us to Children's Hospital immediately! Sam, I'm so scared. Please come with me!"

Sam calmly said, "Honey, this is just a precaution. Dr. Mohan would have hospitalized Chase if it was an emergency. He is doing the right thing because he knows how worried we would be." I felt better hearing his calm reassurance.

When I got to Children's Hospital, I was introduced to a specialist who examined Chase. He decided that the mark was a birthmark, but he wanted to do an EKG just to be safe. He also put a Holter monitor on Chase, which is a special device that records the heartbeat and is monitored by a computer. It gives the doctor an extended picture of the heart rate and patterns. So they glued the little sticky things on my baby's tiny little chest and put a strap around his shoulder to hold the monitor in place and sent us home. Sam and I took Chase back up to Children's Hospital the next day. It was about an hour drive, one way. The doctor examined Chase and removed the monitor. He read the results and said that he didn't find anything unusual. The heart patterns were normal, and Chase appeared to have good blood flow in that leg. We were sent home with a lot more peace of mind.

Sam said, "See, honey, I told you not to get so worked up. Chase is fine, but I'm glad we got him checked."

I said, "I'm so relieved that he's okay. It's good that we had a specialist evaluate him. I feel so much better." I turned around and looked at our precious baby in the back seat and quietly said a prayer of thanks.

As the holidays approached that year, I felt some of the usual dread. But there was also a glimmer of excitement. Life was beginning to return to a new normal. I didn't find it as hard to enjoy Christmas, and it was such a blessing to have Adam and Chase. Sam and I thanked God every day that they were both healthy.

It seems that I nursed each baby longer than the one before. With Adam it was nine months, with Brad it was twelve months, and I was still nursing Chase at sixteen months! Sam often joked, "Are you still going to be breast-feeding him when he starts to school?" Chase had begun to lose interest, and I was starting to wean him when I received some bad news. We were still lying in bed that morning when the phone rang. It was Dr. Trotter.

He said, "Mona, your PAP smear came back abnormal. It is a level three, which indicates pre-cancerous cells on your cervix."

I was shocked! I said, "What are my options?" as Sam listened to the conversation.

Dr. Trotter listed our choices for treatment and said, "You and Sam need to discuss it and call me back with your decision."

I thanked him for calling and rolled over into Sam's arms and began to cry. Sam held me close and said, "I think you should have a hysterectomy. These cells have developed since your last checkup after Chase was born, and that has only been a little over a year ago."

I struggled to hold back the tears. "Sam, that would mean we can never have another child."

He said, "I know, darlin', but it would reduce the risk of you getting cancer later. If we only treat it, the cancerous cells could come back, and I don't want to take a chance on something happening to you."

I knew he was right, and in my heart I had to agree with him. But, it wasn't an easy decision.

We called Dr. Trotter back and scheduled the surgery. Then I called my mother to tell her what had happened and to see if she could come and stay with the boys.

She said, "Of course I'll be there! I would never let you have surgery and me not be there with you."

As the time for my surgery approached, I told the boys, "Mommy has to go into the hospital for a few days, but Mimie is coming to stay with you."

They started yelling, "Mimie is coming! Mimie is coming!" I was happy that they felt comfortable with my mother, and I knew she would take good care of them. That was such a relief, and it allowed me to face the surgery with less anxiety. I was in the hospital for three days. The surgery went well, and I recovered rapidly. But I grieved over losing the ability to have more children. At the age of thirty-three, I had already lost one child and any hope of having another one. It made me even more thankful for Adam and Chase as well as the time I had with Brad.

# THOUGH HE SLAY ME

I had always looked forward to spring and summer, and after losing Brad, I began gardening. It made me feel good to grow things. Seeing new life was so much more pleasant than experiencing death. I went on a mission to grow as many plants as I possibly could. I had started a flowerbed on the west side of our house. It was fairly secluded and shady, and Chase loved to walk through my garden. I taught him to pull the dead flowers off my petunias! We spent hours out there in the spring while Adam was in school. We would work and talk and sing. Mostly, though, I would answer his questions, and those never ended.

As Chase grew and his personality developed, it became clear how funny he was! Sam and Adam would teach him to say things, and he would repeat them word for word. Adam would act like a televangelist and say, "Brothers and sisters! There *is* a ray of hope!" and Chase would say, "A *ray* of hope?" I have no idea where Adam came up with that shtick, but it cracked me up.

Sam taught him to say to me, "Hey, Big Mama." I really didn't like that one. Even my friend Paula would teach him stuff. We would be at Pizza Hut with the church crowd, and Paula would whisper something in Chase's ear. The next thing I knew, Chase would yell out, "*Are you necked, Margaret?*" I wanted to climb under the table.

Once, we had seen Ray Stevens in concert in Branson, and Chase thought he was the funniest man in the world, so it didn't take much to get him going. When the movie *Forrest Gump* came out, Chase would say, "Hi, my name's Forrest Gump. People call me Forrest Gump." He wouldn't pause in his delivery, and he would move his mouth just like Forrest Gump did in the movie. He got some new tennis shoes once, and while we were at the baseball field after a game, Chase said, "I got new tennis shoes. Watch my dust!" and he took off running.

Everybody loved Chase. We introduced Sam's cousin Todd to my friend Julie, and they really hit it off. They were at our house for dinner the first time they met, and Chase was right in the middle of every-thing. Todd and Julie went outside to play basketball, and Chase asked me, "Are they gonna kiss, Mommy?" Then he headed outside to keep an eye on them. He was their little chaperone! It didn't deter the rela-tionship because they ended up getting married in a few months. As their marriage vows were being said, Chase leaned over to me and said, "Are they gonna kiss, Mommy?" I think we all realized how blessed we were to have Adam and Chase. God had truly answered our prayers and restored some of our joy.

Brad's death date, March 15, came and went each year with a little less emotion, but the grief was felt just as deeply. We never wanted to forget him, so we always acknowledged those special anniversaries and tried to talk about the time we had with him. I especially didn't want Adam to forget his brother. When Chase passed his third birthday, I think we all breathed a sigh of relief. In the back of our minds, that was a marker. If he got past that, he would be okay. These weren't rational fears; we had no reason to think anything would happen to Chase, or even to Adam, but our human hearts couldn't forget the pain. We knew we couldn't survive it again. I can remember praying and asking God, "Please let me keep Chase." But in my heart, I knew I had to be willing to give him up. Everything we love has to be placed upon the altar, and we have to trust God. Just like Abraham laid Isaac on the altar, there are no guarantees in life. Something could happen to any of my family. Would I still trust God? I prayed that I wouldn't have to face that test.

My mother and sister came up for spring break in March. A new children's museum had opened in Seminole, and we were excited about taking the kids there. At eleven and seven years of age, Adam and Hollie were at the perfect age to enjoy the museum, but there was an obvious gap in their ages—someone was missing. Hollie and Brad had been so close. Madalyn was already five, and Chase was about to have his fifth birthday in May, so they were best friends. Mother, Tara, and I were worn out after keeping up with them. Of course, they wanted to go back every day! We had a fun week that had to end too soon because school would start again on Monday.

Toward the end of March, Sam had to go to Houston on a business trip. The Sunday before his scheduled trip, he decided to take Adam and Chase fishing. They bought some live worms for bait, loaded the boat on the trailer, and away they went. Sam took them to a farm pond where he knew they would catch something. When they got home that evening, they had caught a few, but Sam said it was more fun just baiting Chase's hook and letting him catch little perch.

Chase ran into the house and said, "Mom! We went perch jerkin'! Dad would put a worm on my hook, and every time I threw it into the water, I would catch a little fish!"

Sam described how Adam had a blast running the trolling motor and steering the boat. I was so glad they had fun together, but I was just a little envious. It must be wonderful being a dad and sharing moments like that with your sons. I guess I would never know how that felt.

Adam was in school that Wednesday, and Chase and I made a trip to Walmart. You guessed it: to buy more flowers. Spring was arriving quickly, and I had to get started planting soon. As I walked through the garden center, Chase was jumping around, and I was afraid he would fall or knock something over, so I picked him up and put him on my hip. He grabbed my face and pulled it to him and said, "No more flowers, Mommy. No more flowers!" I could take a hint, and Sam was due to be back from Houston anyway, so we left Walmart and headed for home. As we left the parking lot, we saw Vicki Yates from church and her children, Luke and Emily. Chase waved to them through the window as we drove past them.

We got home and were out in the yard when Sam pulled into the driveway. Chase saw Sam's pickup and began yelling, "He's home! Dad's home!" and went running out to meet him. Sam grabbed Chase and picked him up and gave him a big bear hug. "How is my buddy?" he asked.

"Did you bring us anything, Dad?" asked Chase.

"Well, I don't know. Let's go inside and we'll see," Sam said as he winked at me. We all went into the house and sat down to visit about the trip to Houston. Adam was home by that time, and it was good to have everybody together again. I never felt quite right when someone was missing.

As we were talking, Chase began to get bored with the adult conversation, and he asked, "Mom, can I go outside and ride my bike?" He was allowed to ride just so far, and he was very good about staying within those boundaries, so I said, "Okay, honey, but be careful," thinking that I would go out and check on him in a few minutes. Chase bounced down from Sam's lap and ran out the back door. Adam went to watch television in the other room, and Sam and I continued our conversation.

"How was your trip?" I asked.

"It was okay, Sam replied. "But, I sure am glad to be home."

All of a sudden, the doorbell rang. It kept ringing and ringing. Sam and I jumped up to see who was playing with the doorbell. It was Michael, a young man from church. He said, "Chase has been hurt. Call an ambulance." Sam ran outside, and I tried to grab the phone. Then I pushed the panic alarm on our security system. I couldn't remember the number for the ambulance; I looked it up. The phone rang. It was an elderly lady from church. I told her, "I can't talk right now!" and tried to get off the phone, but she kept talking. Finally, I said, "I've got to go." And hung up the phone. Then I called for the ambulance. I screamed into the phone, "Hurry, I don't know what happened! It's our little boy!" And I gave them our address. Then I ran outside. In my heart, I didn't want to go out there because I was terrified of what I would see. I found our little son lying on his back and, Tandi, a friend from church, was giving him mouth-to-mouth resuscitation. Sam was standing to one side, and people had gathered all around. Our house was right across the street from the church, and people stopped to see what had happened. I looked up and saw Adam as he dropped to his knees and yelled, "No, God! Not my brother! Please, not my brother!" I thought I was going to pass out. I saw people staring at us all. It was like we were in slow motion again. I went over to Chase, and I could tell his eyes were fixed and dilated. I had seen that look before.

A newspaper photographer snapped a picture of Chase, and someone yelled at him to stop. He said, "Hey, I'm just doing my job." A policeman had arrived, and then the ambulance came. They loaded Chase onto a stretcher and took him to the hospital. Sam and I jumped into his truck and followed the ambulance to the hospital.

When we arrived at the emergency room, it seemed surreal. I felt like I was reliving a nightmare. Surely this was just déjà vu. This couldn't be happening again. We sat in the same waiting area that we had waited in six years ago. The same friends from church gathered around us. Brother Bob had retired, and we had a new pastor, but he was out of town. It seemed like forever before the doctor came out to talk to us.

I still wasn't sure what had happened. All we knew was that Tandi had been on her way to church, and she looked over and saw Chase lying in our driveway. He was still straddling his bike, and he wasn't moving. Tandi is a nurse so she immediately stopped and began to perform CPR.

The doctor on call happened to be a neighbor of ours, and he walked over to us with a very stern look on his face. He put his arms around Sam and me and said, "We're trying to revive him. We're doing all we can." Then he turned around to leave, and I said, "Doctor, I believe in miracles." He just looked at me and headed back to the emergency room. Sam and I were in shock. Time stood still. We could hear every second as it ticked by. There were no words to say. We just sat silently praying and weeping. I felt like throwing up. I don't know how long we waited.

Finally, the doctor returned. He gathered Sam and me in a room away from the others and said, "I did all I could. I even put a port in his leg to try to give him medication quicker. I tried to restart his heart several times, but he's gone. I'm sorry."

"No! Oh, no! Oh, God! No!" I fell to pieces. Sam grabbed me as we both wrestled with our emotions. It felt like our world had come to an end. How do you go on? How do you accept something like this? We struggled to get our wits about us because we knew we had to see our son for one last time before they took his body away.

As we walked toward the emergency room, there was dead silence except for occasional sobs. We walked past our friends and into the same room where Bradley had laid. There on that cold steel table was our child. He was so still. I knew I was going to spend as much time as I wanted with him. Nobody was going to rush me this time. I pulled the sheet back to look at his little body. I wanted to memorize every inch. He was bigger than little Brad. Chase was almost five years old. He was my "big boy." His skin felt cold and rubbery, and his lips had a blue tint. Sam and I just stood there studying our son; the child we loved was not there. It was just a lifeless shell, because his spirit had already gone. Sam and I both knew that Chase's spirit was with the Lord. We spent some time just holding one another and looking at what was left of our child. Finally, we kissed him on the forehead and slowly walked out the door, closing it behind us.

We felt like we were riding on a float in a very sad parade. As we walked past our friends with their tear-streaked faces, we got a few hugs, and we headed out to our truck to go home.

As we turned into our driveway, I saw images of what had happened earlier that afternoon. My mind replayed every incident in slow motion as I tried to accept the reality of what had happened. We were still in shock. I think God allows us to go through shock because we could not physically or emotionally deal with such a devastating trauma all at once. People describe it as "walking through molasses." Everything slows down. You can't hurry or get in a rush because your mind can't function in that capacity. Your memory is foggy, and you keep trying to figure out what actually happened. I call it God's shock absorber, because it gives your body time to adjust. But, even more than that, it gives your mind time to accept—gradually—what is happening.

# FAMILY PHOTOS

Brad - age 14 months        Adam - age 4
Time for bed and prayers on our knees.
A special time that only God sees.

Adam - 4 yrs.        Brad - 2 yrs.
Torn tee shirts and old army hats.

Adam - age 6

Adam - age 11    Chase - age 4           Chase - age 4
                                    Practicing his football pose.

Chase's "Pog"

Tiffany and Adam,
Ethan and Austin

Mona and Austin - age 4 months,
Sam and Ethan - age 19 months

# BROKEN DREAMS

It's hard to explain, even now, as I relive these events, but Chase died on a Wednesday evening in March, just as Brad had. Both times it was around the time for church services to begin, so many people became aware of what had happened right away and began gathering at our house. In God's grace, he brought people around us to help care for Adam and take care of Sam and me. This time, Erica, a friend from church, arrived at our house that night and stayed from morning until night for days. She said God impressed upon her heart that she needed to be there. She was especially good to Adam. Having four grown children (two of which were boys), she was very sensitive to what he needed.

One of the hardest things for me to do was call my mother and tell her what had happened. She was devastated by Brad's death, and I was afraid this would be more than she could take. To make matters worse, she had been to the dentist the day before to have several teeth extracted. I knew she was physically weak, but she had to be told. I decided to call my cousin's wife, Angela, who was the secretary for Mother's church. She could reach the pastor, and, since it was a Wednesday evening, they would be meeting for church. That would be the best place for Mother to receive the news. So Angela called the pastor and my mother's sister to prepare them for what had to be done. When they gathered for church that evening, my mother arrived and walked into the sanctuary. She saw them all together and immediately asked, "What's wrong? Has something happened?" They told her that Chase had died, and she collapsed into a pew.

We had to figure out a way to get Mother to Oklahoma as soon as possible. She needed to be with us, and she needed to hold Adam. Unbelievably, Neal, another friend from church, stepped forward and offered to fly to Arkansas and get her and my aunt Florene that night. Dale, who managed the airport, made a private plane available, and Neal flew down to Texarkana. I have no idea who paid for all of this, but what a blessing.

My memory of that evening is very foggy. I just remember sitting in my living room and having lots of people around. I remember feeling so sad in my heart and telling one of my friends how sorry I was for putting them through this again. We had been the benefactors of such gracious generosity and love; but how many people ask their friends and family to support them through the same horrible experience again so soon? In my heart, I feared that people would think I wasn't a good mother or that we abused our children. I fully expected the police or DHS to come and conduct an investigation. Normal people just don't go through things like this. And then the most traumatic possibility of all came to mind. Most marriages don't survive the loss of one child; what were the chances of ours surviving now?

My mother finally arrived late that evening. She was barely coherent from the shock of it all. I just remember her being very weak and frail. Her mouth was sore from the dental extraction, and she couldn't eat. She had never liked to fly, but that had not even been an issue because she was so grateful to be with us. That's just the way a mother is; she wants to be there to comfort her children. Ironic, isn't it? I wasn't able to comfort mine.

Gus brought us some medication to help us sleep. I refused to take it because I remembered how it made me feel before. My mind was muddled enough, and my life felt so out of control. I didn't want anything to dull my senses. As awful as it was, I wanted to be able to feel. That's the only way I could tell I wasn't dead. We fell into bed that night, exhausted with grief, and slept.

The next morning, I remember waking up, and the light was streaming into our room. Once again, I felt the ton of bricks land squarely on my chest, and my stomach began that wretched aching that started in my gut and spread up my chest to my throat and down into my bowels. I felt immobilized. Only my mind was racing—remembering—and then it started; that howling guttural groan of grief. As Sam rolled over to hold me close, I could feel the ache in his heart, but men don't cry, so I wept for both of us. Then, when he couldn't contain it any longer, the floodgates opened. We lay there trying to come to grips with what had happened.

We couldn't think about the future. We just had to make it through today. Sam reassured me that the Lord would be with us. We just had to trust Him.

Someone heard that we were awake, and Erica or my mother came in to check on us. People had already started gathering at our home, and our closest friends were allowed to come back to our bedroom to see us. The first person I remember seeing was Brother Bob. In his usual quiet and gentle way, he reassured us that the Lord would not leave us or forsake us at this time. He told us he loved us, and then he prayed with us as we lay motionless on our bed.

I remember our longtime friends Steve and Jacquie coming by. Steve sat on the bed with tears in his eyes as he fumbled for words to say. I told him about the worms that were still in the refrigerator—the ones that Chase had used to catch fish with the Sunday before. Sam and Steve were old fishing buddies, and I knew he would appreciate the significance. We visited for a few minutes, and then Sam asked Steve to be a pallbearer, again.

While we were still lying in bed, Erica came into our room to tell me that my mother had passed out. My heart jumped into my throat! Erica explained that she had collapsed in the living room but appeared to be okay. She hadn't been able to eat because of the dental surgery, and she was very weak. But, just to be on the safe side, Gus was coming by to check her. As it turned out, our suspicions were correct, and she felt stronger after we forced her to drink some broth and eat whatever else Erica could get down her.

Our dear friend Doug Melton came early that morning. I could tell he was brokenhearted over our loss because his son, Zachary, and Chase were best friends. Doug was their baseball coach and had held their first practice on Tuesday night. At that time, Doug was dean of students at Oklahoma Baptist University, but from Wednesday until Saturday, he barely left our side. I started calling him my shadow. He just wanted to comfort us, and I think it helped him to be with us too. That's one interesting thing about grief. People want so much to help you carry your burden of grief, and they feel better just being able to be there for you. I think it helps them work through the grief process as well.

# YET, WILL I TRUST HIM

S am and I were like zombies. We were the walking dead, just going through the motions and trying to make necessary decisions as best we could. At least this time we knew what had to be done. Sam went about making the funeral arrangements. Once again, I went and helped him pick out the casket and flowers. This time, the choices were easier. We certainly knew the ropes. We even knew how much funerals cost.

I got out my family pictures and spread them across the dining room table. My mother and I spent hours gleaning through them to find the pictures we wanted to display at the funeral. We tried to choose the ones that told the story of Chase's short life. I take a lot of pictures, and it was very hard to pick only a few. But, gradually, a mosaic of Chase's little life appeared.

Our new pastor, Kelvin Moseley, (everybody called him Pastor K) returned from a revival in North Carolina and came by to comfort us and begin preparations for the funeral service. He met with us to talk about Chase's life and our memories of him. It seemed appropriate to sit in Chase's bedroom as we reminisced about the time we had with our son. After a couple of hours, we had given the pastor enough information to prepare the eulogy. I had to tell Sam and Kelvin what God was speaking to me in my heart. Since Chase's death on Wednesday, I had the feeling that I wanted to say something at Chase's funeral. I was so concerned that people would think we were angry and bitter. Most people knew about our loss of Brad six years earlier, and I wanted them to see the peace of God that Sam and I had and to tell them about Christ. I wasn't sure I would be strong enough to do it, so Kelvin said he would look at me, and I could shake my head yes if I wanted to come forward. We agreed on that signal, and we prayed that God would show me what to say.

Sam and I had five employees who needed their paychecks, so I had to get payroll done on Friday, the day before Chase's funeral. I couldn't focus, and my mind felt like it was floating in the clouds. My aunt Florene tried to help me, but it was something that I had to do myself. She helped me check it to make sure I didn't make any mistakes, and we finally got it finished. I'm sure it took me twice as long as usual, but our employees were amazed that I got it done. They were expecting to have to wait a few days, and they were very grateful when we called them to come pick up their checks.

There was the usual trip to the funeral home to view the body and to make sure Chase looked all right. I had chosen to dress him in the clothes he wore to Todd and Julie's wedding. He looked so handsome. Karen Green took pictures because I knew I couldn't take it all in at the time.

I had been praying continuously to the Lord to show me what He would have me say at the memorial service. Nothing specific had come to my mind until I woke up the day of the funeral. I kept thinking of a scripture that I had memorized before, but I couldn't remember where to find it in the Bible. I could barely remember my name at that point, so I called my friend Cynthia, Brother Bob's daughter. She couldn't think of it either, which is unusual because she has memorized many scriptures. I'm sure she was not thinking clearly either, so she called her dad. It was Galatians 2:20 (KJV), "I am crucified with Christ; nevertheless I live."

Chase's memorial service was held later that Saturday morning. Adam had requested that his friend Jeff be allowed to sit with the family. Chase had been crazy about all of Adam's friends, and they all loved Chase. I thought it would be good for Adam to have the support of a friend, so, of course I agreed. Once again, our family gathered together at the house in preparation for the service, and I requested that we all join hands and pray. Then we quietly walked down the driveway past the very spot where Chase had died and across the street to the church.

As I entered the sanctuary, I smelled the familiar aroma of fresh flowers. There were dozens of beautiful bouquets spread across the front of the altar, and there in the middle of them was the tiny white casket that held our son.

I approached the casket carefully and arranged some of his toys that were displayed. The large pictorial display was on an easel next to the coffin. I noticed the familiar sounds of organ music in the background.

We walked back to the holding room where the rest of the family was waiting until time for the service to start. I noticed that my sister was conspicuously absent. She didn't sit with the family at Brad's funeral, and I just assumed she was emotional and didn't want anyone to see her crying. Soon one of the funeral directors came and got us, and we lined up to walk into the sanctuary and take our seats. It felt like déjà vu as we filed into the sanctuary just as we had six years earlier.

Before a word was spoken, we heard the voice of our friend Johnnie Mae Foxx pierce the silence with "Amazing Grace." There was no music, just Johnnie's soulful voice calling us to focus on Christ and to remember his saving grace—"Through many dangers, toils, and snares I have already come / 'Tis Grace that brought me safe thus far, and Grace will lead me home."

Then, our music director, David Gibson, led the congregation in singing "Amazing Grace" in unison. It was the most beautiful sound as our bare souls stood before God, and, even in our grief, we praised and worshiped our creator.

Pastor K walked to the microphone and directed everyone to the scripture on the back of the bulletin. We read the 23rd Psalm in unison.

> The LORD is my shepherd; I shall not want. He maketh me to lie down in green pastures: he leadeth me beside the still waters. He restoreth

my soul: he leadeth me in the paths of right-
eousness for his name's sake. Yea, though I
walk through the valley of the shadow of death,
I will fear no evil: for thou art with me; thy rod
and thy staff they comfort me. Thou prepar-
est a table before me in the presence of mine
enemies: thou anointest my head with oil; my
cup runneth over. Surely goodness and mercy
shall follow me all the days of my life: and I will
dwell in the house of the LORD forever.

He then prayed, "Thank you Lord that you are our refuge and our strength, an ever present help in the day of
trouble, our life, and our salvation. Father, you are holding this family in the shadow of your wings. We have
come together today to remember a beautiful, precious
little boy. We have also come to remember your Son,
whom you gave for our lives. So Spirit of God, speak
to each of our hearts and comfort us. In Jesus's name.
Amen."

A longtime friend and church member stepped to
the microphone and sang a song that summed up what
we all felt. "When Answers Aren't Enough, There is
Jesus." "And your heart will find a safe and peaceful
refuge. / When answers aren't enough, He is there."

Our pastor emeritus, Brother Bob Hammons,
stepped to the podium. It seemed so natural for him to
be there as he had been so many times before. He first
referenced 2 Corinthians 1:2-4 (KJV),

Grace be to you and peace from God our Father,
and from the Lord Jesus Christ. Blessed be

God, even the Father of our Lord Jesus Christ, the Father of mercies, and the God of all comfort; Who comforteth us in all our tribulation, that we may be able to comfort them which are in any trouble, by the comfort wherewith we ourselves are comforted of God.

He began by saying, "The reason I have chosen this passage of scripture dates back to September of 1989. Mona brought to me a poem that she had written. It was one of the sweetest, most blessed poems that I had ever seen in my life. It was such a blessing to me. It was an expression of what they had felt since the events of March of 1989. In that poem, she used passages of verses from that passage of Scripture about the wonderful comfort of God, and how through His comfort, they have been able to comfort others. I won't read the entire poem today, but I want to read just the last four lines. I'm sure it will touch your heart very deeply as it does mine even as I reread it today."

Then one day, I began to realize
as I looked at this through the Father's eyes.
We're still a family of four, full of love
There are three of us here and one up above.

That poem is still as true today as it was
then, but we must change the last line…

"We're still a family of five, full of love
There are three of us here, and two up above."

Brother Bob looked down at Sam and me with compassion as he said, "I want you to know, Sam and Mona, how much all of us love you. We are all in prayer to the Lord Jesus Christ for you. You are in our prayers and in our hearts in a most special way. Adam, we want you to know that you are such a blessing to your parents. Grandparents, may God reach down and touch you in a very special way."

Sam and I had asked Janice Campbell to sing "Peace in the Valley" again, just as she had done at Brad's funeral six years earlier. She stepped to the microphone and began the familiar song that had touched our hearts so deeply before.

When Janice finished singing, there were tears on every face. Pastor K stepped to the podium and began the eulogy, "Our hearts have been deeply touched by this service and blessed. I'm especially thankful today that Brother Bob could be here and share his heart with us. We are gathered to worship together and remember. It's amazing that a little boy like Chase Adkisson could bring us all together like this. I know that his family wants you to know how deeply they appreciate the expressions of love that you have demonstrated. I am thankful not only for the response of this church family but to many others who have been touched by this family's grief. Chase Adkisson's life and his untimely death have united this entire community. You know, it's in times like these that you find out who your friends really are. You have a church full of friends and family, Sam and Mona, and more who would be here if they could."

Sam and I were very aware of Adam's reaction as he listened to Pastor K continue, "There are a lot of questions that surround Chase's death, and we've already heard a song that addressed some of those questions. When answers aren't enough, there is Jesus. When our hearts are overwhelmed with grief, there is peace in the valley. There is peace in the midst of the storm. I received the news of Chase's untimely death when I was preaching in a revival meeting in North Carolina. I preached on the second coming of Christ as I fought through the tears. I had about two hours during the drive back to my parents' home that evening. We cried a lot and prayed a lot, and during that process, God gave us a word. My heart went to the eleventh chapter of John's gospel. For there, the Holy Spirit reveals to us both the deity of Christ and the humanity of Christ. We also see the pain of a family in grief—Lazarus and Martha and Mary. Two sisters whose hearts were broken because their brother had died. In his perfect timing, Jesus comes to minister in a crisis. The deity of Christ is revealed in verse twenty-five (KJV) where Jesus declares: 'I am the resurrection, and the life: he that believeth in me, though he were dead, yet shall he live.' Those words took on new meaning when Jesus came out of that tomb. His humanity is so crystal clear in the shortest verse in the Bible. John 11:35 (KJV)—'Jesus wept.' In his humanity, he loved Lazarus." I felt numb as I tried to focus on the beautiful words of Scripture that Pastor K quoted.

"Chase lived one thousand seven hundred and eighty-two days of life upon this earth. An awfully brief span of time, but he packed a lot of life into those few days. There are some things about Chase that you may not know. If you were around him any length of time, you would know that Chase loved ball—all kinds of ball. When he was still in diapers, his daddy gave him a baseball and a football and began teaching him to play ball. Last Tuesday night, Chase had his very first baseball practice. He was fielding balls, and it was cold that night. While he caught balls with one hand, he had the other one in his pocket trying to keep it warm. But it was okay with Chase because he was excited about being on the baseball team. Chase had already practiced how he would stand for his photo sessions. He had a baseball pose and a football pose. He had already shown his mother how he planned to stand with one foot on the soccer ball for that picture. He loved to watch Adam and his friends play basketball. Recently at a basketball game, when the team came pouring out of the dressing room onto the floor, at the end of the line was Chase, fully dressed in a basketball uniform. He was ready to play. His mother had to drag him off the floor so the game could begin."

I looked over at Adam and Jeff. Huge tears were rolling down their faces as they recalled the incident that Pastor K described. My heart was aching, and I began to feel that guttural moan that was now so familiar. It was then that I felt Sam's firm embrace, and as I looked up at him, I felt Adam rub my arm.

I knew the time was coming when Pastor K would look at me to see if I was strong enough to come to the podium. I tried to evaluate myself, but I just wasn't sure

I could do it. Then I heard Pastor K as he continued to speak. "I listened to Brad's service, and something Brother Bob said is true again today. We will never regret the fact that Chase lived. How blessed we've been to know him, even in the brevity of it. Chase is living today. He's living in Jesus. I know you mommies and daddies are trying to understand it. It's hard for adults too. But we must remember that he's safe in the arms of Jesus. In Scripture, we see that Jesus brings the children to himself. Today in heaven he may have Brad on one knee and Chase on the other. All of the things his parents provided for him are now being provided by Jesus. He will never be sick again; he'll have no hunger or pain. There'll be no sorrow or grief like we're feeling today. The little body before us is Chase's little tabernacle. In Second Corinthians, Paul calls the human body a tabernacle. Chase left his little tabernacle behind. He doesn't need it anymore. He is absent from the body but present with the Lord. Like David in the Bible, we can't bring him back, but we can go to be with him."

At this point in the service, Pastor K read a poem that someone had written about Chase:

> When I think of Chase, I think of love,
> The kind that Jesus knew
> Not on hand when it all began,
> But I loved him through and through.
> When I think of Chase, I think of kindness,
> For he showed it in every way.

Gentle and tender, he clearly showed
it throughout the day.
When I think of Chase, I think of smiles,
The jokes, the laughter, and joy.
He was all Chase, all Sam and Mona's heart
Wrapped up in one little boy.
When I think of Chase, I think of friends.
The kind we need to be today.
He treated you right and helped you share
And was always ready to play.
When I think of Chase, I think of Jesus,
And now Chase is with him to stay.
Oh, victory in Jesus, we'll see
them both again someday.

I still don't know who wrote the poem, but it had to be someone who knew Chase well because it described his personality beautifully. I couldn't help but remember how blessed I had been to be his mother—even for only four years. I felt Sam's arm around me as he continued to comfort me, but I could tell he was struggling to keep his composure too.

"We hurt today, but Jesus cares," continued Pastor K. "He sympathizes with our pain. Jesus is living today. He is the resurrection and the life. The difference between Christianity and all other world religions: Jesus lives. Because he lives, we can face tomorrow. Chase is preaching a sermon today." Then Kelvin told one of Sam's favorite stories about Chase.

"One of the favorite things in our Sunday morning services is the Mystery Box time. When I came to this church as pastor, I brought a wooden box that is about a foot wide and a foot tall. During the children's sermon, I gather the boys and girls around the altar in the front of the church. Each Sunday, one of the children gets to take it home and fill it with things that are precious to them. Chase got to take it home one day. When he brought it back, it was filled to the brim with a Sooner football helmet, balls, and all kinds of things." Sam and Adam laughed out loud as they recalled Chase and the Mystery Box. "I wonder what Chase would put in the box today?" Kelvin asked. "He's had some hours in heaven now. What would he put in the box?"

"I think he would put three things in the box. I think he would put *faith* in the box—that's the only way his family is going to make it. Trust in the Lord with all your heart. In all your ways acknowledge Him, and He will direct your paths. It sure is hard to trust in God when events like this happen. Sometimes when you try to harmonize the character of God and cir-cumstances, it leads to confusion. But, God's character doesn't change. He is love, He is kind, He is good. He's the same yesterday, today, and forever. Someone has said, 'When you can't trace God's hand, you can trust His heart.'

"Chase would put *hope* in the box. We're grieving today, but not as those who have no hope. We grieve with the hope that God is in control. We possess living hope that someday we will see Chase again." Hope— that was something I could use a lot of right then.

Kelvin continued, "I think Chase would put *love* in the box. We should be called the children of God

Romans 8:37-39 (NIV) asks the question that is on everybody's mind today, 'Who or what can separate us from the love of God?' "In all these things we are more than conquerors through Him who loved us. For I am convinced that neither death nor life, neither angels nor demons, neither the present nor the future, nor any powers, neither height nor depth, nor anything else in all creation, will be able to separate us from the love of God that is in Christ Jesus our Lord." These are eternal treasures that will not fade away.

"Finally, in the box there would be a few messages for Mona and Sam. Life is a gift. Daddies, don't forget that the life of your children is a gift. Life is precious, and it's fragile. Second, heaven is a beautiful place. If Chase could send us a postcard, it would say, 'Wish you were here, it's a beautiful place. Mom, I'm having a great time. Wish you were here.' And the last message would say,' eternal life is the greatest gift! The most tragic thing that could happen is for people to leave this service today without responding to God's gift of love. You see, God loved the world and gave his only son. Whoever believes in him shall never perish, but will have everlasting life. Chase is preaching a powerful sermon today. Chase is where we want to be. That's the only way these parents and grandparents are making it."

At this point in the service, Kelvin looked at me to see if I was able to speak. I shook my head yes, and Sam stepped forward to help me up the steps to the podium. As I walked up to the platform, my knees were weak and trembling, but I felt compelled to say what God had laid upon my heart.

"Thank you for grieving with us. Thank you for your love, prayers, and support. We will need it in the days ahead. We've tried to raise our children in a Christian home and in the nurture and admonition of the Lord. We haven't been perfect parents, but we've done the best we knew how to do. I know we all question, 'Why would God, whom we love, allow this to happen?' I don't have an answer for that. But I want you all to know that I'm not standing here in my own strength. Galatians 2:20 (NIV) says, 'I am crucified with Christ: nevertheless I live; yet not I, but Christ lives in me: and the life which I now live in the flesh I live by the faith of the Son of God, who loved me, and gave himself for me.'

"It's not me who is able to stand and talk to you today. It's the Lord. The God that we serve is alive, and He cares about us. In spite of this tragedy, the worst legacy we could leave for my family and my sons would be if you were to walk away angry and bitter. I want you to remember that the best thing Chase could receive and the best thing my family could receive would be for each of you to be able to face God unafraid. Please remember that my life was changed in a heartbeat, (as I snapped my fingers) just like that. The only way to prepare for something like this is to draw close to God. The only way to make it through this kind of trial is to have a relationship with Him. He's real, and he's personal. I know Him well; we've walked this path before.

"I don't know how God placed us in such a wonderful church. Your outpouring of love has been unbelievable. I love you all. Thank you." Then, Sam stepped forward once again to help me as I slowly went back to my seat.

Pastor K stepped back to the podium and asked everyone to join him in prayer. He said, "If anyone has never asked Jesus to come into their heart, please do that now." He didn't ask anyone to come down the aisle but to pray and ask God to help them live every day for Him. He asked moms and dads to pray that they would cherish their homes and their children. If anyone made a decision, he asked that they please share that with Sam or Mona or the family. He prayed that those who didn't know Christ would trust Him for the very first time. He prayed they would be a good support system for us in the months ahead.

Then came the time that I had dreaded so much. The funeral director led people to file past Chase's casket for one last time. As our family sat on the front row, people began to hug us and speak words of sorrow as they passed by. It seemed to take forever, and sometimes we would stand up to make it easier. Then we would get tired and sit down. Sometimes my knees felt weak, and I could hardly stand. It was encouraging to feel the warmth of hugs and know that people were so touched by Chase's life.

I didn't realize it at the time, but later, as I watched the video of the service, I noticed that Adam would often reach over and hug me. He would pat me on the arm or brush my hair from my face. It was precious to me to see him being so kind and loving. Often when people would hug him, he would pat them on the back as if to comfort them. Sometimes he would take his glasses off and wipe the tears from his eyes. His friend Jeff sat motionless the whole time. Adam would reach over and give him a hug or pat him on the back.

Finally it was time for the family to say their good-byes. As each one filed past the casket and spoke to us, there were tears of sadness. Devin had a particularly difficult time. He broke down in tears as Sam tried to comfort him. My sister walked up to the casket and almost collapsed. Roger helped her back to her seat as my mother and father walked up there. Then someone helped Sam's mother wheel over in her wheelchair. Adam and Jeff stood there and looked at Chase for a long time. Adam comforted others as best he could. It's hard to relive the brokenness of those moments. Our suffering was compounded by seeing those we loved go through this again. After everyone else had left, Sam and I spent a few moments with our son. We wept as Sam held me in his arms and tried to comfort me. I leaned over and kissed Chase's forehead for the last time.

# THE DARKER SIDE OF GRIEF

I don't remember Chase's graveside service. I don't remember much at all after the funeral, just flashes of the faces of people and fragments of conversations.

One scene that I'll never forget is sitting at the kitchen counter talking to people and turning to look behind me only to see my brother-in-law Roger sitting there with tears streaming down his face. Roger is a big guy, and I had never seen him cry. He was probably reliving the time last summer when Chase and Adam stayed with him and Tara. They had taken a video of Chase and Roger playing ball in the yard. I'm sure every parent did just as Pastor K had instructed. They went home and held their own children a little tighter that night.

Tara and Roger's oldest daughter, Hollie, was Brad's age, and she was too young to know what was going on when he died. But she had lots of questions now. I remember standing in the living room as Hollie looked at me and said, "Why wasn't anyone watching Chase while he rode his bike?"

I felt anxious because I was afraid to tell them the details of what had happened. I said, "I often let Chase ride his bike in the driveway. He knew exactly how far to go and I would always check on him." Their youngest daughter, Madalyn, was just a few months older than Chase, and I'm sure she was also wondering what had happened to Chase. I tried to answer their questions the best way I could without frightening them any more than they already were. Thank goodness they seemed satisfied with my answers.

Many family members had to leave right away, but a few stayed for a couple of days. Our church family once again stepped in to support us and minister to us in unbelievable ways. Several people provided sleeping arrangements for family members from out of town. Many continued to bring food for two weeks or more, and some would stop by to check on us periodically. We received cards in the mail for months. Although my mother hated to leave us, even she had responsibilities to tend to. So after a few weeks, she went back to Arkansas.

Adam's friends had surrounded him immediately upon hearing of our ordeal, and they continued to come to our house after school and on weekends. It was almost as if they needed us as much as we needed them. There were mornings when I would walk into the family room and find Michael, Matthew, Chris, and Jeff asleep on pallets or sprawled out on the couch. As I watched them sleep, it brought tears to my eyes as I thought of the hurt they must be feeling. Their innocence had been shattered like a baseball hitting a glass window. It happened suddenly, and there was no way to reverse the damage.

I was thankful that Adam had people like Erica to talk to, and I was hoping that he was able to express the grief I knew he felt. The memory of him dropping to his knees and praying to God in our driveway the day Chase died haunted me, and I was sure it haunted him too. His cries were etched in my mind, and the sound of them echoed in my soul.

We got the autopsy results fairly quickly this time. It clearly showed that Chase's neck had been broken at C1 vertebrae. It also showed scratches on the top of one hand, indicating that he had not tried to break the fall. This was consistent with a neighbor's account of what she witnessed. He had fallen face down and never tried to stop himself or jump off his bike. Chase was very athletic, and we felt sure that he must have died before he hit the ground. Otherwise, he would have jumped off the bicycle or at least put his hands out to try and catch himself.

Once again, Sam and I struggled to come to terms with what had happened. We were in shock for weeks. I don't think we began to feel the full impact of Chase's death for a while. Fortunately for Sam, he had a new business opportunity presented that he began pursuing immediately. But I was left to face the cold silence of an empty house. As the days went by and the realization that we would have to face the future without two of our children began to sink in, I became very depressed. I would sleep until Sam came home for lunch, then I would go back to bed and sleep all afternoon. At times,

I would be lying in bed and hear the distinct sound of Chase's rollerblades on the tile in the hallway, and my heart would skip a beat.

There was actually a great deal of physical pain involved in my grief experience this time. I felt a heaviness in my chest that seemed unbearable. The emotional pain was so intense that I asked God to let me die. But the pain fell just short of death. I have to admit that the thought of ending it all crossed my mind. Although it would have ended my present suffering, such a selfish act would have destroyed Sam and Adam as well as my mother and sister. During those times of deep despair, I got a glimpse of what Jesus must have felt when he cried in Matthew 27:46 (KJV), "My God, My God, why hast thou forsaken me?"

Grief isolates like no other experience on earth. I couldn't allow the pain I carried to be inflicted upon others. Hot, boiling tears were always there, just beneath the surface, steeped in the agony of suffering. No family member, not even my husband, who more than anyone else understood what I felt, deserved the full force of my soul-wracking tears.

Satan did his best to convince me that God didn't really care. I felt like I was in a spiritual battle with God sitting on one shoulder and Satan sitting on the other. Just as I would proclaim the hope of seeing my children again someday, Satan would whisper, "You don't really believe that fairytale, do you?" I often quoted one of my favorite scriptures at those times. 2 Timothy 1:7 (KJV), "For God hath not given us the spirit of fear; but of power, and of love, and of a sound mind."

I read as much and as often as I could. That seemed to be the only way I could keep my focus on the eternal perspective. As wonderful as it seemed to live eternally in heaven with my family, it didn't quench the longing in my heart to hold my children and my dreams.

I cried out to God for answers. Why did this happen *again*? Had we not passed this test once already? We had praised God in spite of our suffering, and we had placed our trust completely in Him. Is this the result? Why did He ask us to have faith if He was going to crush that faith again and again? My testimony used to be that God carried me through the suffering of grief and then restored me. What would my testimony be now?

It was easy to become self-absorbed. Not only had I lost my children, I had lost my identity. I was once an active wife and mother who ran a business and taught Sunday school. Now I felt paralyzed. I couldn't get outside of myself long enough to give to my husband in the ways that he needed me to. No longer did I have an adoring four-year-old whose face lit up when he saw me. Now I had an only child; a twelve-year-old who craved independence. Before Chase's death, I had felt the awesome presence and power of the Holy Spirit in my teaching, I now felt crushed in my spirit and abandoned.

Almost exactly two weeks after Chase's death, the bombing of the Murrah Federal Building in Oklahoma City occurred. I couldn't watch TV because the images of children being dragged from the building were just more than I could handle. As if that weren't enough, I got a notice from the IRS that we were being audited.

Even the day-to-day activities of life were difficult. My body and mind were in shock, my memory was foggy, and it was hard to stay on task. The things that once seemed so important now seemed irrelevant. Paying bills and buying groceries became monumental tasks, and the very act of performing those tasks brought back the feeling of loss. Paying the hospital and funeral bills placed another peg in my son's coffin. It was final. When I bought groceries, the nagging feeling that I had forgotten something was always with me. As I stood in the checkout line, I would catch myself looking down to make sure Chase was by my side.

In spite of my lingering depression, life went on. Because of my inability to concentrate, the business began to suffer. I dreaded keeping up with payroll and taxes; therefore, I procrastinated and would end up feeling guilty as the work piled up. We owned a retail business that required me to see people, so I only worked when I absolutely had to. I preferred to stay in bed, and I did as often as I possibly could.

My prayer was that God would give me the faith that I needed to survive and come through this ordeal in a way that would be pleasing to him. I have read that when circumstances look bleak, it is good to look back at the times God has answered our prayers and brought good out of bad situations. The Bible says in 2 Corinthians 4:17-18 (KJV),

> For our light affliction, which is but for a
> moment, worketh for us a far more exceeding

and eternal weight of glory; while we look not
at the things which are seen, but at the things
which are not seen: for the things which are
seen are temporal; but the things which are not
seen are eternal.

The pressure to place a proper monument at Chase's
grave weighed heavily on me. I was sure people who
drove by the cemetery wondered why there was only
a plastic marker there. That and the fear of losing our
memories of Chase prompted me to write another
poem. I wanted his legacy to be etched in stone just
like his brother's, so instead of working, I spent hours
laboring over every word. There is very limited space
on a headstone, so each phrase had to be meaningful. I just can't explain how difficult it was for me to
determine what aspects of my son's life deserved to be
memorialized. Months later, we ordered the headstone
and had this poem inscribed on the back.

# IN MEMORY OF NATHANIEL CHASE ADKISSON

## MAY 2, 1990-MARCH 29, 1995

Merciful God's precious gift of love
Came straight from Heaven so far up above.
Delivered by Angels; A ray of hope,
My baby, Chase, to help us cope.

He was all boy…just ask Adam, his brother!
Oh, how they grew to love one another.
We again learned to laugh and play away the hours.
Chase loved the garden and watering my flowers.

Chase was "cool," hardly ever any trouble.
He could ride a bike, rollerblade, and even blow a bubble!
These moments were treasured deep in a mother's heart,
Always aware that we, too, must part.

He said we were "the best family in the whole wide world."
We could hardly believe it when God's plan was unfurled.
A familiar experience; the end of a dream,
No more football poses; no more baseball team.

Another Wednesday evening, God's family would appear
Only to be told that Chase isn't here.
Revisited by sudden death, that mysterious chill,
Again God whispered, "Peace, be still."

# NEVERTHELESS, I LIVE

Our days on Earth are numbered, for some there are so few.
Dear, Brad, how he loved you, now Chase is in Heaven, too.
  Absent from the body, but present with the Lord.
  Chase dropped his toys to pick up the King's sword!

  He was swooped into Heaven on cherubim wings.
  "O Victory In Jesus!" Are the words his heart sings!
God's mystery box is opened…its contents poured out.
  The angels are rejoicing! Did I hear Bradley shout?

Death, where is thy victory, O, death, where is thy sting?
  Though our hearts are sad, our spirits sing!
  The Father is watching from Heaven up above
  Jesus is weeping with a heart full of love.

  The Holy Spirit is praying, as only he can do.
The Prince of Peace is present, to help see us through.
  We're still a family of five full of love.
  God's grace is sufficient, but we long to be above.

Mother

# THE MIRACLE
# OF FAITH

S am and I realized that we needed to be proactive regarding Adam's health. If there was even the remotest chance that something could happen to him, we wanted to know it. We made arrangements through our pediatrician for an appointment at Children's Hospital to consult with a pediatric electrocardiologist. He conducted a series of tests on Adam that took some time. The doctor even did a study that entailed monitoring Adam's heart while injecting him with epinephrine. This caused his heart to fibrillate as the doctor watched it on a sonogram.

After extensive testing, the doctor assured us that Adam was healthy. He said, "I can continue to test Adam for years, or you can choose to give him a normal life." He also told us that he suspected our sons who died had some sort of recessive genetic trait. We could do genetic testing on Adam, but at that time it was extremely expensive. Besides, even if we found a problem, it wasn't likely that we could do anything about it. So we opted to take Adam home and do our best to give him a normal life.

When I saw the doctor for my annual checkup, I confided in him how depressed I was. He assured me that I wasn't going crazy; it was a normal reaction to tremendous stress. He said the multiple traumatic experiences that I had endured likely had depleted my brain of necessary chemicals. He prescribed an anti-depressant and suggested that I begin taking it immediately. I got the prescription filled and took a pill the next morning, but it made me feel jittery inside, so I didn't take it again.

Time passed slowly. The annual birthdays and events came and went without much notice. But that year, I dreaded Christmas more than ever. As the inevitable day approached, Adam sensed my extra dose of sadness. I'll never forget walking into my living room one afternoon, and there were Adam and Jeff hanging ornaments on a Christmas tree. Tears trickled from my eyes as I realized they were doing it so I wouldn't have to.

My sister and I talked on the phone occasionally, and I could tell she was struggling with anger over what had happened to me. During one of those conversations I tried to gently tell her to trust God. I could hear Tara sobbing as she blurted out, "I'm pregnant, Mona! I didn't want to tell you because I knew it would have to hurt you again. Not only that, but it's a boy."

My heart skipped a beat as the realization of what she was saying sunk in. "Tara, that's great. I'm happy for you."

She said, "But you won't want to come around us because it will remind you of the boys. I know it will be hard for you."

I said, "Of course it will remind me of my boys, but it will also remind me of how precious they were. God will give me the grace to deal with it. Please don't let my sadness diminish your happiness. I wouldn't want that to be the legacy my children leave." She agreed to try to enjoy her pregnancy and look forward to having her first son.

Sam and I knew that Christmas would never be the same, but we still wanted to make it special for Adam, so we decided to begin a new tradition. We took a ski trip that year around Christmas and allowed Adam to invite Jeff to go with us. We went to Red River, New Mexico, and rented a condo. The boys had a blast, and Sam and I tried our hand at snow skiing for the first time. It felt good to get some exercise, and the fresh mountain air was invigorating. I remember standing on the top of a ski slope with snow falling on my face. I could see for miles, and the view of the mountains was breathtaking.

I stayed on the bunny slopes for the most part, but Sam accidentally got on a black slope. He actually did pretty well, but about halfway down he hit an icy spot, and his right knee buckled. He came down the rest of the way really fast—in a dog sled pulled by an emergency rescuer. When we got back to Oklahoma, he went to the doctor and found out he had torn his ACL and needed surgery, which he had right away.

Then he spent the next two months recovering and doing rehabilitation.

As if that weren't enough, Sam had some huge issues come to light in his new business that required board members to vote one of the partners out. This placed a great deal of stress on my husband, because he would be required to fulfill the obligations he had made to investors without the human resources he thought were available to him. It also alienated the former partner and his family we were very close to. We met with them to pray together in an effort to salvage the relationship. Unfortunately, they chose not to reconcile. Sam and I were both very sad that we lost their friendship, but we can honestly say that we tried our best to redeem the situation.

As the first anniversary of Chase's death approached, I knew it was going to be difficult. The seventh year anniversary of Brad's death passed on March 15, and as the 29th drew closer, I could feel my spirit sinking. By the time that date arrived, I was a basket case, and I began taking the antidepressants I had been prescribed. After a few days, the strange feeling they gave me had subsided, and they seemed to take the edge off my emotional episodes. I took them for about six months.

My sister began to have some problems during her pregnancy. She was diagnosed with a panic disorder that was debilitating at times. Her doctor told her it was caused by the fear that her son might die the way Brad and Chase had died. I told her, "Tara, God is in control, and you cannot allow anger to take hold of you. I know it's hard to understand why he allowed this to happen to us twice, but if you become angry and bitter, then Satan will have victory in your life. God can use this tragedy for good if we will trust him."

She said, "I just don't get why He let this to happen, not once, but *twice*?" I could hear the emotion in her voice as she held back the tears. "I can't stand to see you go through this again. It breaks my heart!"

I began to cry as I heard the pain in her heart. "I don't understand either, Tara, but I know God is good, and he wants the very best for his children. If we can't trust him through this, then how can we trust him at all? We will never know *why* this happened until we are in heaven some day and God reveals it to us. But we have to remain faithful to Him now, even though we don't understand. I don't want the death of my boys to give Satan any victory. If he can cause us to doubt God, then we will be full of fear and anxiety over the future. God wants us to have peace in spite of our circumstances, and the only way to have that peace is to trust him. Philippians chapter four verse seven says, 'and the peace of God, which surpasses all understanding, will guard your hearts and minds through Christ Jesus' (NKJV). I believe that with all of my heart because I'm experiencing that peace. Of course I have my moments of discouragement, but instead of turning away from God, I run to him as fast as I can. Just like a little child that climbs into her daddy's lap when she's afraid."

A little over a year after Chase's death, Tara delivered a healthy baby boy that she named Matthew Kolt Beckham. Her irrational fear caused her to be overprotective of all of her children, but especially her son. I counseled her many times to let go of her fears, and she finally confessed to me that she hated God for what had happened to me. I told her that if she turned her back on God, Satan would get the victory. I think that made her see things in a different light, and she did finally confess her anger to God and repent. Unfortunately, the panic attacks continued.

The hardest thing for me to understand was why God seemed so silent. I longed for the comfort I had felt in the past, but it just wouldn't come. I cried out to God in my prayers for answers; still, He remained silent. Maybe I didn't have enough faith; maybe God sensed my anger and was disappointed in me.

I turned to the book of Job. If there was anyone who could understand what I was going through, it would have to be Job. As he faced one trial after another, Job never lost faith in God. It was reassuring to read that even though God was silent much of the time, He was aware of Job's suffering from the start. I felt like such a weak Christian, but even in my times of doubt, I sought God. The very cries of my heart were a yearning for fellowship and reassurance from Him. As I often say, I would rather hang on to God in the darkness than walk alone in the light. Once again, I poured my heart out on paper.

# THE MIRACLE OF FAITH

Father of mercy, please hear my prayer;
I need your grace, and to know that you care.

My heart is so troubled; I must plead my case
Like Job of old, as I fall on my face.

Lord, you know the desires of my heart.
Still I cry out...but where do I start?

Oh, Lord! I'm wounded...this pain I can't bear!
Do you not hear me? Lord, don't you care?

How long must I suffer through this living death?
Wouldn't it be better to draw my last breath

Than to see those I love be consumed with such pain
To live may be Christ, but to die is great gain!

Questions are unanswered, as if no one's there.
Lord, are you listening? Do you hear my prayer?

Your love will spare me this suffering, I know!
My heart can't survive this torturous blow!

Give me a miracle! Show your mighty hand!
But God only knows the lessons he's planned.

As I hear Christ whisper the words that he said
To those who followed the miracles I've read.

"I've already worked many miracles for you
What will it take for your faith to come through?

Signs and wonders might help you believe,
But if they don't come, how long will you grieve?

# NEVERTHELESS, I LIVE

If only you'd trust me, the dark wouldn't stay.
Just hold my hand never ceasing to pray.

Child, learn to walk by faith, not by sight
Trusting my Father to make all things right."

Faith comes from hearing the true Word of God.
His love is so clear as my memory I prod.

Jesus saved me from death and the penalty of sin.
As I opened my heart, His Spirit came in.

If that isn't miracle enough to convince,
I remember the peace I've known ever since.

The circumstances of life may cause us to doubt.
Isn't suffering and loss what the cross was about?

God understands our pain and suffering reviled.
His swan song of grief was the loss of a child.

"Why hast thou forsaken me?" Jesus cried from the cross.
Yet God chose to leave him through suffering and loss.

When we don't understand and our minds can't conceive,
We can't see his hand; trust His heart and believe.

This, too, has been sifted through His hand of love.
Our treasures aren't here; they're stored up above.

So I'll press on to the mark and finish the race.
His strength flows through weakness as I walk in His grace.

The Lord of hope gives me strength to love while I can
With faith as my miracle, I trust God's perfect plan.

Mona Adkisson

# MONUMENTS AND MEMENTOS

Grief makes getting through your day-to-day routine very difficult. Even the most practical daily activities are a challenge. Not only is your body and mind in shock, but your memory is foggy, and it's hard to stay on task. It feels like time is standing still, and things that once seemed so important are irrelevant. It's hard to pay bills and buy groceries when your mind is reliving the pain and loss that you feel. It's almost impossible to stay focused.

The first time that I had to do laundry after each death was painful. With every article of clothing I folded, I was reminded that I would never get to do their laundry again. It's funny how something as simple as a pair of socks can take on so much significance. I remember when Brad died, friends came rushing to our home to help. Without giving it a thought, they quickly gathered all the dirty clothes and washed them so I wouldn't have to. They never realized that those dirty clothes contained the last scent that I would ever smell of my son. I was terribly sad when I became aware that his aroma was gone. I did find stuffed animals and a few things that contained a faint smell, but his clothes and even the sheets he had slept on the night before were washed clean.

How was I to know that dirty clothes were important? I had no idea. But when Chase passed away, the first thing I told people was, "I appreciate your help, but please don't touch anything. Sam and I need some time with his things before they're moved." No one did his laundry, and they didn't even pick his toys up in the back yard. Everything was left exactly as he had left it. We had the rest of our lives for cleaning and putting things away, and it gave Sam and me the opportunity to see and touch and smell the last physical evidence that our son had lived.

I took a few articles of clothing, some special toys, drawings, and cards from Chase and placed them in a plastic box under my bed right next to the one that had been there for six years. In my nightstand next to my bed, I still have a few articles of clothing that remind me of my sons. Sometimes, if I hold them really close to my face, I can catch the faint scent of a little boy.

When Brad died, most of his things were passed on to Chase. But after Chase died, I really struggled with what to do with his clothes and toys. There were a few things that I knew I would never part with, but there were many other things that I knew some other child could use. I just couldn't bring myself to give anything away. I felt guilty, but for months Chase's room remained just as it had been. Sam tried his best to get me to go through Chase's things and give them to someone in need, but I wasn't ready to part with anything that reminded me of him. I had recently redecorated Chase's room with his favorite Disney character, Mickey Mouse. It had been a huge surprise, and he loved it. But now, Mickey Mouse was frozen in time. The rocking chair that held such sweet memories sat very still; his rollerblades lay tossed in his closet. I would often lay on his bed and weep. Then I would slowly walk to the door as I looked around the room, taking in the deafening silence, and quietly close the door behind me.

Nothing was changed for over a year. It bothered Sam, and he often mentioned it, "Mona, we need to do something with that room. How long are you going to leave it like that?"

"I can't, Sam! I've tried, but I just can't do it right now!" I would get angry if he tried to push me to get rid of anything. "Do you want to go through his things," I would ask? "No, you don't," I would answer my own question, "So just give me more time! I'll do it soon. I promise." I grieved so deeply, and he seemed to want to rush through it. I know he felt the pain as much as I did, but he just handled it differently. His business kept him focused on new problems and new opportunities while I spent every day steeped in memories of my two precious boys. Adam had turned twelve years old and was so independent. He seemed to have adjusted fairly well, although I worried because he didn't want to talk about what had happened to his brothers.

I finally became convinced that I should not make a shrine to my children. I went to Sam and said, "I realize that God desires our worship for Him alone, and not even our children can take His place. I'm going to try to put Chase's things away."

He said, "Honey, I'm so glad, and I know you'll feel better once you're done,"

I couldn't help but feel guilty for dragging it out for him as well as for myself. I began, "I'm sorry it's taken me so long—" as Sam cut me off.

"I know it's not easy, darlin'. Just do as much as you can each day."

Tears welled up in my eyes and then spilled down my cheeks as I felt his strong arms around me. He was ready to move on and so was I. It had taken me a long time, but I was finally convinced that moving forward and trying to put our life back together didn't mean that I would forget my children or that I loved them any less. It simply meant that I had to do everything I could to redeem the time I had left with my remaining family.

I gradually went through the toys and sorted them into boxes to give away. The ones with special memories were placed in boxes and labeled, but I still couldn't bear to put them in the attic. So they were stored in the top of Chase's closet. It took many months before I actually went through his clothes and personal items. Chase's baseball team had given us the trophy they had won, and it remained on the top shelf of his closet, along with his baseball and glove, even after the room was redecorated several years later.

One way I have preserved the memories I cherish is by having the VHS videotapes I had made through the years transferred onto DVDs. Now I can watch them on my computer or play them on the TV. I don't watch them often, but occasionally, on one of their birthdays, we'll watch them. I'm so grateful that we have this technology now.

I would encourage anyone who loses a family member to try to journal their thoughts and feelings. I did it sporadically through the years, but I wish I had been more consistent. It's enlightening to go back and read what I was thinking and feeling. It can also be a form of therapy. You can express your thoughts without fear of condemnation, and it helps you to work through the grief process.

# SWEET DREAMS

My heart was broken, and I dreaded the future. But God in his goodness saw my pain and provided reassurance in the most unexpected ways. About a month after Brad's death, I had a dream. In it I walked into the boys' room and reached into the crib and picked my son up. I had a strange feeling that something was wrong. I was afraid that his head would flop because his neck couldn't hold it upright. But as I held him close, I could see that he was fine! His eyes were bright and healthy. He looked into my face and smiled. I plopped him on my hip and ran down the hallway into our bedroom to tell Sam, "Brad is okay! There is nothing wrong with him! He's fine." I couldn't believe it! The dream seemed so real. My arms that ached to hold my son were now embracing him with love. I had longed to feel the texture of his skin, and now I was actually rubbing his arms and legs. They felt so soft and smooth, just the way I remembered.

When I woke up, I was a little sad to realize it had only been a dream. But even more than that, I was happy that I had the chance to hold my son one more time. God has allowed me to dream about my children many times since then. It's usually around their birthdays. Most of the time, I dream about one or the other of them, but occasionally, I'll dream about them both.

My dreams are never sad or tragic. They usually involve me playing with them or talking to them. Sometimes I can't touch them, or they won't respond to me. But that is rare. Most of the time, I wake up feeling like I've been with them all night, and we've shared some very precious time together.

My mother tells me that she too dreams about my boys. She often plays with them in her dreams and wakes up feeling like she has really been with them. It is comforting to be able to see them and hear them and to occasionally be able to touch them.

God has comforted me through dreams of my children, but He has also comforted me in other ways. I remember one time when I was really struggling to accept Brad's death. I was at the cemetery, and I prayed asking God to show me that Brad was okay. As I stood there facing his grave, I looked up, and in the clouds I saw the distinct image of Mary and Joseph holding baby Jesus. Behind them stood a cloud of witnesses. My heart melted as I accepted the answer to my prayer. Brad was with many people who loved him; who better to watch over him than the earthly parents of Jesus, our Savior?

God has answered many of my prayers. Even though I struggled desperately to accept the loss of my boys, God never left me. At times I felt alone, but I realize now that He was there all the time. I just couldn't feel it because of the pain and grief I was experiencing. In my darkest hours, He really did carry me. When I didn't think I could face another day, His strength flowed through my weakness. As the beautiful Twenty-Third Psalm says, "Yea, though I walk through the valley of the shadow of death, I will fear no evil, for thou art with me..."

One of the most precious acts of love that I have received from God was after Chase died. I was at church on a Wednesday night and just happened to be standing outside the nursery where my boys had spent many hours. I had a coat on that I had worn for years, and as I placed my hand in my pocket, I felt something inside. As I pulled the object from my pocket, I realized that it was a small round disc that belonged to Chase. It was what the kids called a Pog. As memories came flooding back, I rolled the disc over and read what was written on it. As I did, my heart skipped a beat! I couldn't believe what it said: "Soaring High with God."

# THE ETERNAL PERSPECTIVE

One evening at Walmart, I happened to see a lady from church. I almost didn't recognize her because she was driving a handicap cart and wearing a turban. She called me by name, and as I began walking closer, I realized who she was. We had been in a Bible study together a few months before. As we chatted, she said, "I've just finished my sixth chemotherapy treatment. God is so good. I have a loving husband who has been wonderful during this difficult time. I also feel blessed that my friends from church drop by for a few minutes or they call me on the phone to check on me."

I said, "Oh, I'm so glad you've had so much support. We all need that, don't we?"

She heartily agreed, and she said that my mother-in-law, who was her neighbor at the time, had come by for a brief visit. I couldn't help but sense the peace and serenity that this woman had. She didn't once mention her pain or discomfort. Her eyes literally lit up as she talked about the Lord and how he had ministered to her. This woman was truly grateful to be alive.

Illness often triggers the grief process because it brings you face to face with the possibility of death. A loss of any kind can cause us to grieve. Whether it is the loss of a job, the loss of a pet, a financial reversal, or the loss of a precious child, our natural reaction is to experience some form of the stages of grief. Each of us must choose how we will respond to the tragedies we face in life. We can succumb to our emotions and allow them to sink our will to live, or we can look for God's greater purpose. Yes, I believe that God can use all of our circumstances to mold us and shape us into his image. Amazingly, we are most often transformed in our pain rather than in our prosperity.

We've all pondered the question of why God allows pain and suffering. He could give us a world free of trials if he chose to. Why did he ever allow sin and sickness to enter into existence? He could have prevented the fall of man if he had chosen to intervene. I read a devotion recently by the late, great pastor, Dr. Adrian Rogers. He said that if we lived in a world free of pain, we might never be compelled to turn to God.

When we have everything under control, we don't see a need for a savior. God, in his divine wisdom, knew that without pain, most of us would never appreciate the blessings we receive every day. It is in our time of need that we search for a power greater than ourselves. Some people turn to God and find peace in the midst of their suffering and trials, and some people become angry and bitter. It is at these crossroads of life that we often choose whether we will follow God into victory or deny his existence and trudge ahead, bullheaded, on our own. God gives each of us a choice. We can place our faith and trust in him or we can deny him and live life on our own terms. The consequences of our choices are significant. If we choose to know Jesus Christ as our Savior, we have the hope of eternal life, and this world is just our temporary home.

As I write this, a number of years have passed since the deaths of my two boys. A lot has happened in the lives of people I care deeply about, especially the friends who walked through the valley of grief with us. My friend Cynthia contracted breast cancer a few years ago and underwent chemotherapy. She successfully passed the five-year mark, but two years later, doctors found cancer in her bones. She has undergone a couple of rounds of radiation and recently began chemotherapy again. She continues to boldly witness for Christ and is an inspiration to those who know and love her.

Her two sons, Matthew and Daniel, are both married now. Matt is in seminary getting his doctorate and has a heart for ministering to the Chinese people. He was the youth/English pastor of a Chinese church in Oklahoma City for a couple of years. It's amazing, isn't it? Because his SCIDS (Severe Combined Immune Deficiency Syndrome) went undiagnosed for the first year of his life and he almost died, Cynthia was planning his funeral. But God had other plans for Matt.

Daniel and his wife have a beautiful baby boy, and he is now a successful financial advisor with a national firm. Cynthia's two daughters each have children with SCIDS because the gene is carried only through females. Although they cannot contract it themselves, it is passed on to their male children. This amazing family still trusts God and uses every opportunity to witness to others about His goodness and mercy. They continue to turn their tragedies into triumphs.

Our friends Ken and Karen Green had two beautiful children of their own, Kenny Ray and Krista. Kenny, their oldest child, was diagnosed with Ehlers Danlos Syndrome, a connective tissue disorder, when he was a child. Several times I've received a call from Karen saying, "We're at the hospital. Kenny has internal bleeding, so he will have to undergo another surgery."

The last time it happened she cried, "We almost lost him. The next major organ to go will probably be his aorta."

You couldn't tell there was anything wrong with Kenny by looking at him, but the disease caused the tissue of many of his organs to be weak and to tear easily requiring extensive surgery. But each time Kenny bounced back with more determination to squeeze as much life out of each day as he possibly could. He seemed fine, but he almost gave his mother a heart attack on multiple occasions!

Sadly, Kenny Ray Green died in a small plane crash at the age of twenty-two. It felt surreal as we attended the funeral of the child of friends who had been such a support to us as we buried our own children. Ken and Karen still trust God and see His hand at work in their lives. Kenny's prognosis had not been good, and they take comfort in knowing that he lived his life to the fullest up to the very last minute.

We all learned a lot about how to truly live by watching Kenny Green overcome his circumstances time and time again. He accomplished so much in his short life. He became an Eagle Scout in spite of his limitations. Kenny never focused on what he couldn't do. Instead, he set out to accomplish everything he could dream up. At the time of his death, Kenny was a firefighter and sought training at every opportunity to be the very best he could be. He had worked his way up to the captain of his firefighting unit. Having learned to fly at an early age, Kenny soloed before he got his driver's license at the age of sixteen! What an accomplishment! Unfortunately, the surgeries he underwent caused him to stop flying for a number of years, and he was just beginning to pick it up again. Ironically, Kenny was not the pilot that day; he was a passenger. A family friend was piloting the plane and suffered a traumatic brain injury in the crash. He and his family continue to walk the path of pain and suffering, but they are sustained by the grace of God and the prayers and support of Christian friends and family.

My son Adam is a grown man now. Even before he was born, I prayed for him to find a Christian wife, and God has certainly answered that prayer. I have a wonderful relationship with his beautiful wife, Tiffany. Before they married, I felt that I needed to prepare her for the reality that what had happened to us could potentially happen to her and Adam. When I brought the subject up to Tiffany, she said, "I know, Mona. Adam and I have discussed it. We know that it's possible for the same thing to happen to us. But we also know that whatever the future holds, God will take care of us, just as He has you and Sam." What a blessing! There was no debate about the possibilities. There was no crying or dread in her voice. Only the calm assurance that their faith in God would be their strength and that they would trust Him no matter what their future might hold.

Yes, Christians suffer just like everybody else. The difference is that we have hope because of our faith in Jesus Christ as our Savior, which helps us keep an eternal perspective. The world we live in is full of adversity and pain. Only when we view life through our spiritual eyes can we see the world as God intended it to be. Psalm 19:1 (NIV) says, "The heavens declare the glory of God; the skies proclaim the work of his hands." Although we live in a fallen world, we can have joy if we focus on the eternal perspective. We must look past the troubles of this world and view our future as it is— held in the hands of God.

# A FUTURE OF HOPE

Because of the loss of two of our children, we have learned to treasure each day. We try to be generous with the "I love yous" because we never know when it will be the last opportunity to tell our friends and loved ones how we feel. After all, the only real legacy any of us leave is the love we give to those around us. Maya Angelou is credited with the saying, "I've learned that people will forget what you said, people will forget what you did, but people will never forget how you made them feel."

Brother Bob taught me years ago to pray before I get out of bed in the morning, "Lord, help me live this day for you." That is a good habit to practice. If you focus your heart and mind on pleasing the Lord, you are better prepared to meet the challenges of the day, whatever they may be. No matter how difficult life becomes, God has a way of giving us hope if we look to him in prayer. His Scriptures are full of verses about hope.

"For I know the plans I have for you, declares the Lord, plans to prosper you and not to harm you, plans to give you hope and a future" Jeremiah 29:11 (NIV).

Romans 15:13 (NIV) says, "May the God of hope fill you with all joy and peace as you trust in him, so that you may overflow with hope by the power of the Holy Spirit."

"Be joyful in hope, patient in affliction, faithful in prayer" Romans 12:12 (NIV).

> Therefore, since we have been justified through faith, we have peace with God through our Lord Jesus Christ, through whom we have gained access by faith into this grace in which we now stand. And we boast in the hope of the glory of God. Not only so, but we also glory in our sufferings, because we know that suffering produces perseverance; perseverance, character; and character, hope. And hope does not put us to shame, because God's love has been poured out into our hearts through the Holy Spirit, who has been given to us.
>
> Romans 5:1-5 (NIV)

The last couple of years have been amazing for Sam and me as we've experienced the births of our grandchildren. Adam and his wife, Tiffany, have been blessed with two sons, Samuel Ethan and Nathaniel Austin. They were both born with dark hair and the most beautiful blue eyes I've ever seen. The love I feel for them is indescribable. I began praying for both boys before they were born, and I know that God has an amazing future in store for each of them. Adam has tentatively agreed to a third child, and Tiffany is hoping for two more, but they are praying for God's direction.

Sam and I have been blessed with successful business ventures and spend much of our time traveling between them. God has given us tremendous opportunities to share our story and tell others about the hope that we have in Christ. I've included some resources in the last chapter of this book which others may find helpful. We would not have guessed at the time of our losses that our sons' lives could have touched so many people. But God in his wisdom has used our circumstances to spread the good news that there is hope *in Christ*.

# A DATE WITH MOM

As I reflect on the time I had with my sons, there are so many things I wish I could have told them. Sudden death robbed me of the opportunity to tell my boys good-bye, so I would like to end this book with a letter written from me—to them.

"Hello, boys—this is your mother. I'm not sure you remember the sound of my voice, but I feel certain that you remember how much I love you. Our time together on earth was so short, but we sure packed a lot of living into the time we shared. Your dad and I have so many wonderful memories, and we still talk about you often. We remember your smiles and hugs. We remember so many cute things you did and all of the funny things you said. Your brother, Adam, misses you too. Yes, it's been a long time, but we still remember you, and we want you to know that we'll never, ever forget either of you.

I miss you both, and sometimes my heart aches to hold you. It would be so nice to be able to talk to you and to see how much you've changed. But I want you both to know that, as much as I long for you, I would never wish you back. I know by faith that you are in the presence of God and that no evil can ever touch you there. I picture you walking together with Jesus in perfect peace and contentment. There is no more sorrow there and no more tears. You will never know the suffering that we do here on earth because your bodies are whole and healthy.

I thank God that he chose me to be your mother. You both blessed my life beyond measure, and I'm a better person for having known you. Thank you for the love you gave so freely and the joy that you brought to everyone around you.

Someday, when my time on earth is finished and the Lord calls me home, I'll see you again. There will be a reunion that day—God promised! Until then, remember, boys—we have a date.

Love, Mom

# ADVICE AND RESOURCES

When I lost my children, I struggled to find good information about the grief process. Whether you are grieving or you are walking through the grief process with a friend or loved one, the following information will be helpful. Remember to save the platitudes and just walk beside the grieving person or as the Bible says in Romans 12:15, "... weep with those who weep." Listen to the grieving person, even when their thoughts and feelings don't make sense. Remember, they are trying to process what has happened, and they need time to adjust, both mentally as well as physically, to the reality of the situation.

I found comfort in writing my thoughts and feelings in a journal and through writing poetry. Even if the grieving person doesn't feel that they have any writing ability, encourage them to keep a journal. Just getting their thoughts and feelings out on paper will be therapeutic. They will find later that it has been helpful because their memories will fade, but they will have the events permanently documented. Secondly, they will appreciate the ability to go back and re-experience their thoughts and feelings as they work through the grief process.

Contrary to what most people think, grief isn't a one-time event that has a beginning and an end. It typically begins with shock and denial then moves to anger. After anger most people experience denial where they just can't believe what has happened and they don't want to accept it. As the reality of the situation sinks in, depression often results. The final stage of grief is acceptance as life takes on a new normal, but many people don't transition smoothly from one phase to the next. Often they take two steps forward and three steps back as they revert to anger or denial again. Sometimes they get stuck in depression. Everyone grieves differently, but it helps to have an understanding of the process.

I would encourage you to seek help and support. The best place to find local resources is through your church. Many pastors are trained in counseling, or they can direct you to others who are. Often churches offer grief support groups where people who have been through grief themselves can offer help and encouragement to those who are more recently bereaved.

I would caution anyone exploring the internet on the subject of grief. As with every topic, the Internet offers some great information regarding grief, but it also offers damaging or confusing information as well. The resources I have listed below are some that I found trustworthy and should be very helpful.

Here are books that I would recommend:

- *Don't Take My Grief Away From Me* by Doug Manning
- *Facing Death and the Life After* by Billy Graham

- *When God Doesn't Make Sense* by James C. Dobson
- *Choosing to SEE: A Journey of Struggle and Hope* by Mary Beth Chapman
- *The Power of Suffering* by John MacArthur, Jr.
- *A Grief Observed* by C.S. Lewis and Madeleine L'Engle
- *Where Is God When It Hurts?* by Philip Yancey
- *Disappointment with God* by Philip Yancey

*GriefShare*™ seminars and support groups are led by people who understand what you are going through and want to help. Many churches offer GriefShare programs where you'll gain access to valuable resources to help you recover from your loss and look forward to rebuilding your life. There are thousands of GriefShare grief recovery support groups meeting throughout the United States, Canada, and in over ten other countries. To find a group near you, visit their website: www.griefshare.org

*DivorceCare* is a divorce recovery support group where you can find help and healing for the hurt of separation and divorce. You can find where they are meeting at: www.divorcecare.org

*Financial Peace University* presented by Dave Ramsey encourages people to stop worrying about money and instead to get organized to pay off debt as they save for the future. Start your journey to financial peace by finding a local group through the website: www.daveramsey.com/fpu/home

*Focus on the Family* is a ministry that I would heartily recommend not only for grief support but for anyone seeking information regarding all aspects of family life. They offer valuable information regarding everything from marriage and raising children to dealing with financial issues and caring for aging parents or caring for a dying spouse. You can find their website at: www.focusonthefamily.org

*The Compassionate Friends* is a worldwide non-denominational organization which is dedicated to supporting parents who have lost a child. It also offers support to siblings and grandparents through their website: www.compassionatefriends.org

Needless to say, if you or someone you know is grieving, and you feel yourself sinking into despair, please seek help from a counselor or medical professional who is trained to deal with serious mental health issues.

As my experience testifies, it is important for everyone to seek a personal relationship with God, through his Son, Jesus Christ, who died to prove how much he loves us. That truly is the most important and crucial element of dealing with any loss. Grief without God's presence only ends in despair and hopelessness; grief *with* God is no less painful but ends with *hope!*